A Perfect Fish

Illusions in Fly Tying

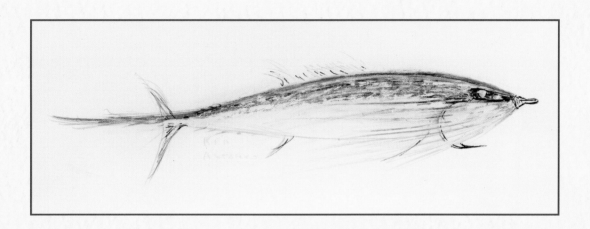

Ken Abrames

Paintings by Ken Abrames

R.L.S. Light Blue

R.L.S. Medium Blue

R.L.S. Indigo

R.L.S. Silver Doctor Blue

R.L.S. Teal

R.L.S. Emerald Green

R.L.S. Light Green

R.L.S. Purple

R.L.S. Dark Blue

R.L.S. Turquoise

R.L.S. Apple Green

R.L.S. Medium Green

R.L.S. Dark Green

R.L.S. Light Violet

R.L.S. Light Olive

R.L.S. Bright Green

R.L.S. Lemon

R.L.S. Medium Yellow

R.L.S. Dark Violet

R.L.S. Medium Violet

R.L.S. Pink

R.L.S. Rose

R.L.S. Beige

R.L.S. Medium Orange

R.L.S. Fuchsia

R.L.S. Red

R.L.S. Fiery Red

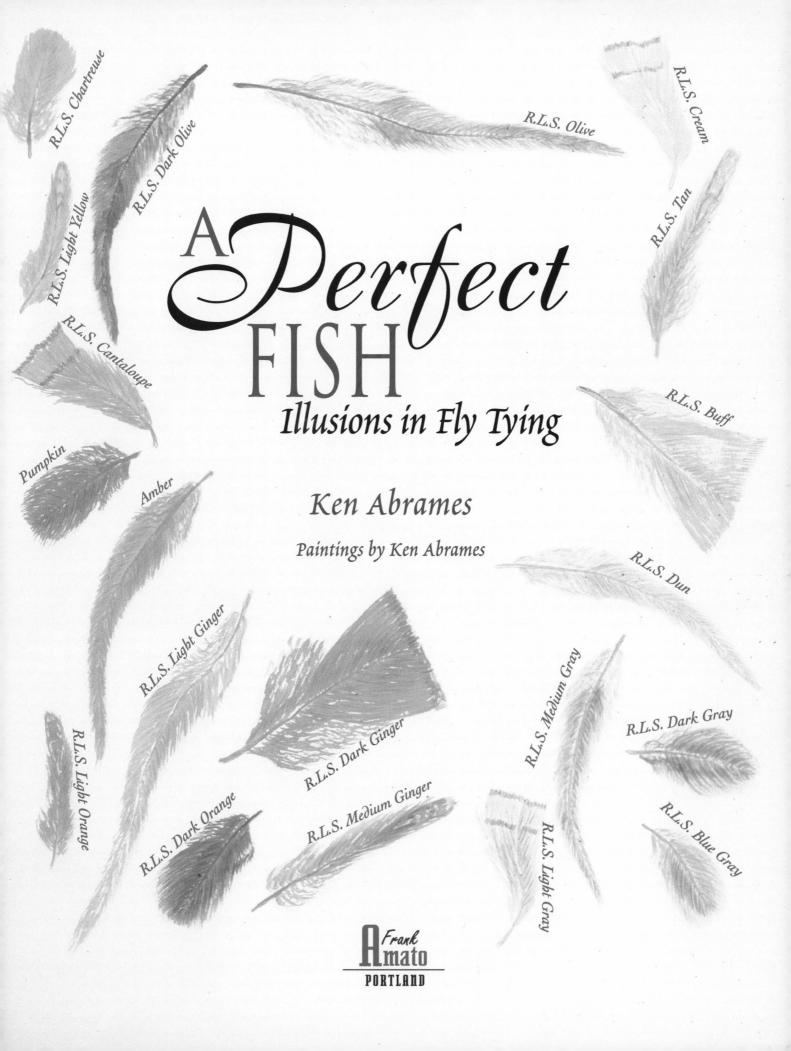

A Perfect FISH
Illusions in Fly Tying

Ken Abrames

Paintings by Ken Abrames

Frank Amato

PORTLAND

R.L.S. Chartreuse

R.L.S. Dark Olive

R.L.S. Olive

R.L.S. Cream

R.L.S. Tan

R.L.S. Light Yellow

R.L.S. Cantaloupe

R.L.S. Buff

Pumpkin

Amber

R.L.S. Dun

R.L.S. Light Ginger

R.L.S. Dark Ginger

R.L.S. Medium Gray

R.L.S. Dark Gray

R.L.S. Light Orange

R.L.S. Dark Orange

R.L.S. Medium Ginger

R.L.S. Light Gray

R.L.S. Blue Gray

To my mother, Edna,
to whom I owe my life,
my daughter Heather, my daughter Maggy Rose,
and my granddaughter Hazel.

ACKNOWLEDGEMENTS
Mark Archambault for his faith,
Al Brewster for his humility,
Pip Winslow for his Spirit,
Kathleen Johnson whose design sense
and encouragement helped make this book a reality.

Andrew Wyeth for sharing with the world his views on creativity and observation.
His awareness touched and sparked much of my own writing in this book.
I am grateful to him for his truth about nature and spirit.
I found his imagery remarkable in its ability to be easily translated
into a fisherman/tier's perception of this mysterious world of angling.
We fishermen have not often looked to the world
of creative expression for the wisdom it offers;
science has been the path most often chosen.
There are other paths to search and perhaps they can provide
new insights and possibilities in our exploration of the natural world.

Joseph Turner, painter, for his exploration of atmosphere within his paintings.
Claude Monet for his use of color, space and light.
Édouard Manet for the beauty of relationship of form and transparance.
Georges Seurat for the science of mechanics translated into beautiful paintings.

And Mary Turrisi for her love of nature, her support and inspiration, and her fire.

Frank Amato Publications, Inc.
P.O. Box 82112, Portland, Oregon 97282
503•653•8108
Paintings by Ken Abrames
Book and Cover Design: Kathy Johnson
Printed in Hong Kong
Softbound: ISBN: 1-57188-138-7   UPC: 0-66066-00338-6
Hardbound: ISBN: 1-57188-179-4   UPC: 0-66066-00381-2
1 3 5 7 9 10 8 6 4 2

Table of Contents

FOREWORD

Kenney Abrames is unlike any fly fisherman I have known. He is unique. Kenney feels deeply about the sport and especially, the striped bass. Most writers will tell you how to tie the correct fly patterns, rig tackle, fight and release fish. But Kenney does it another way. He gives you much needed information, as others do, but he has deep feelings about the sport and fly tying and he shares them. He involves his readers in his way of seeing.

Such is this book. There are wonderful, artistic drawings of many of the best striper flies that he and his friends use. The recipes are there, too, and these flies will catch you fish. More than that, you will comprehend why many flies are not just tied, but created as much from the mind as from the materials.

When you read and study this book, not only will you know how to tie the patterns, but you will understand the striped bass and the soul and mind of those who tie flies to catch this wonderful fish.

—*Lefty Kreh*

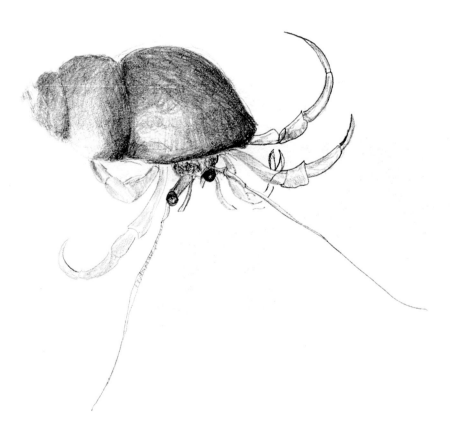

Fly tying is different than fishing.
It is the yeast in the dough
that makes the bread rise.
It adds something magical
to the experience of fishing.
Something indefinable yet understood by all
who sit in front of a vise for the pleasure
of simply tying flies to fish with.
It is a way of touching the core
of who you are as a fisherman.
Your flies show how you think and feel.
They are not just lures they are expressions
of your innermost predilections.
They are gestures of your spirit.
They are statements not possessions.

Fly tying is slightly older than fly fishing.
The first fly had to be tied before
someone fished with it.
I remember sitting as a small boy
and watching with wide-eyed wonder
as my father tied flies and
I remember the first two flies
he showed me how to tie.
They were bucktails.
I even remember the patterns and the hooks.
I still have that vise and my memories.
Thank you Dad.

Flies are personal.
They are like someone's handwriting
or perhaps the way they cook.
There are recipes and languages
but everyone has their own unique way
of understanding and interpreting them.
This book is personal.
There are recipes in it and a language.
Feel free to interpret them uniquely.

—Ken Abrames
May 1998

Roots

I feel a river or a section of surf. I feel it deep within me. All the times I have been just there, in that one place, frees me from being conscious of my surroundings. They are in a very real sense a part of me and because of this I am able to fish from a deeper feeling of what I am doing than I could if I were learning a new place. It is as if the river, the water with all of its complexity, is within me, so in a sense I am fishing all rivers when I am fishing where I know.

I say I love the river, that is my way of expressing the freedom that familiarity opens up to me. I am able to wander and explore endlessly the complexities that are visible to me because I know the river so well. I find a world within the familiar and fishing comes as a natural expression of and through this closeness.

There will be places and moments when my focus will merge and enter in a particular way and then expand and go beyond to explore areas that are connected but can only be reached through the natural slide of insight that relationship engenders.

There are places we care about so completely without conscious appreciation, that we are taken by surprise when our feelings rise to awareness. There are people in our lives of the same order. People and places that we are connected to through such a simple bond that it is hidden by being overlooked, and yet when those connections are altered we feel it profoundly.

There is a boyhood river I fished each spring for trout. It was clear and full of life. There were two branches, one was the natural bed of the river, the other a mill race formed by a holding pond with a sluice and small dam. I fished the natural stream and learned and experienced much of my stream lore there. I saw my first leviathan trout, watched hatches begin, come to fullness and be replaced by the succeeding ones. I experimented with presentation, hooking the fish that rose as the first order of business and through this focus learned the mechanics of fly fishing, and realized in a small way that I had to curb and control my youthful volatility if I was to ever grow in understanding.

One spring my river was no longer there. Someone had built a home on the site of the mill race and altered the water flow to run primarily through the sluice, leaving the natural bed almost non-existent. I did not know how to deal with the feelings that I had. They were of such a magnitude that I would not let myself enter into them. I left the river with a peculiar numbness which I can recall to this day. I can feel those feelings now, that I could not feel then, and even though I would not embrace them then, I know that they had an effect on how I experienced my life from that moment on.

Sometimes it is not a river. It may be a tree that you sit at the base of and read or write. It may be a bench in a park or an old lady who always says hello. It may be an old building that you pass by on your way to a favorite place or it may be an old man you see along the stream who you know has been there in the place he loves and has been connected to, perhaps for his whole life. Seeing him comforts you and you welcome the feeling but do not know that you have it.

Then one day somehow you know he is never coming again and you know the feeling, and you know that the feeling is all you have. The feeling of the old man who sat by the stream is yours and will never leave you and you are glad you have it.

Perhaps it is through feelings that a life is truly lived. I think so. They remain with us long after all the people and places have changed through time. They are timeless doorways to what we have lived. And mysteriously, they are felt with the immediacy of true experience. They are, after all is said and done, the language of our heart.

Fishing is being in relationship with nature, one's own relationship with nature. One can speak and hear it's language best where every blade of grass, each sound and smell, even the look of the place is a part of your history. It is from this familiar touch that deeper levels of yourself are able to resonate. It is like a perfect song that keeps revealing more and more meaning as you ponder it over and over again at different times in your life.

A river I love opens me to these revelations. In the same way, there is a section of rock that juts out in the ocean called Point Judith that I go to both to fish and to simply be. It is the place where my Father showed me the horizon of the open ocean and I first heard and saw its surf. Every time I go there I touch my whole life through an awareness of knowing, of belonging, of being rooted and linked to this earth. It helps me realize that I am connected to so much more than I can ever be conscious of when operating from the functional practicality of my normal awareness. A favorite place is like a path. It can be used as a bridge to the depth within you and this depth is available through the act of simply being there either in one's body, or if need be, through one's imagination. In a sense, it is going home and home is such an ordinary part of the human experience that I am in awe of the simplicity that underlies our seeming complexity.

When I am driving to a place like Point Judith or some river I love to fish, the feeling of being there and the comfort this brings to my spirit sets something free inside of me. I may get an energetic connection to a thought that I have been holding inside, and through this triggering act of going to a familiar place it springs forth in my mind full blown as something I want to try or explore with while fishing. It may be a technique or a pattern in the behavior of baitfish or some such insight and it carries me forward with fresh ideas and determination to learn more about both fishing and myself.

I can do this because my awareness is free, not focused on becoming familiar, but because it is rooted in familiar it goes beyond it and allows me to see. If this detachment is not present one can easily become mired in meticulous attention to details that do not give insight but rather keep one's attention locked on techniques or casting or fly patterns which are actually incidentals or tools, not the essence at all.

What is Fly Tying?

Fly tying is such a huge part of fly fishing that it amazes me that more people do not do it. I do not feel comfortable using flies that other people tie and most of the fly tiers I know feel the same way. There is something solid gained by fishing with your own creations, something personal and satisfying is added every time you catch a fish. It is easy not to tie flies and there are as many reasons not to do it as there are people who don't tie, and perhaps there is only one real reason to do it at all. It feels so good to do that not to do it is to deny yourself access to a wonderful part of fly fishing that is easily within reach.

Flies are expressions of ideas, they are manifestations of someone's insights or fancies or studies in duplication. They are allowed to come into existence best by the one who has the idea and wishes to

sophisticated they may be now, had to start by tying their first fly. The second fly someone ties is always a dramatic improvement over the first and the third fly is often fly tying at its best.

The third fly is a threshold, a masterpiece of imagination. A spark ignites, the fire is lit and someone is home. I have seen it happen so many times that I look forward to witnessing this natural progression with those who tie for the first time. The first fly is all thumbs and self consciousness. The second is trying to get it right, just like the instructions say it should be. The third fly is found when I say to the new tier, "Tie anything you want:" Eyes widen in surprise and uncertainty, confusion sets in, a pause, and then this is followed by "Well, ah, what do you mean, what should I do?" "Anything you want, this place is off-limits to the fly-tying police." Then a smile and then a question. The question is never Why, but always how. "How do I tie a silverside or a herring or a shrimp?" "What do they look like?" I ask. And the spark ignites.

Everyone sees and feels a little differently and this shows in their third fly. It is the magic that holds their attention through their fourth and fiftieth and ten thousand fifty fourth fly. It is what keeps them seeing new things and new ways to imitate these insights and incorporate them into their fly tying and fly fishing repertoire. Fly tying is the endless purposeful exploration of the unknown possibilities that become known to us through opening our awareness to nature's hidden creatures and their interconnected routines.

Fly tying is not only the technique and doing it right, that is a description of the mechanics, of the fixed, of what already exists, of what others had to reach for and find and explore and share. It is a starting point for growth in craft and craft is real but not the fullness of the art. Craft serves the art, it is integral but does not lead to mastery, it leads to replication. It is an important step toward mastery but it is one that has to be subject to your imagination. It is a tool. It is the body of the beast not the being with the spirit to animate it.

At its highest level, fly tying could be viewed as a painterly and sculptural expression of man's reaching out to touch and feel the intangible and make it visible and purposeful, along with simply viewing the beauty it brings to one's eyes and enjoying this as one does a painting of a sunset. It is not Science although it can be dissected and studied and analyzed and categorized. It is not Religion although it does have orthodoxy, devotees, saints and heretics. It is not Philosophy although it has first causes, perception, illusion and truth. What is fly tying? It is nothing more or less than human self expression in relation to a fish and the better you get at expressing yourself, the more fish you can possibly catch. Simplicity itself. All men are equal before fish.

express it. No one can interpret as correctly as the originator. Some tiers tie more beautifully than others but this does not diminish the value of an original idea expressed by a tier of lesser skill. The fly tied by a child will catch fish as will the fly tied by a true creative and expert tier. To not tie because of a lack of expertise is self defeating and has no potential for growth. It is a dead-ended path. Every tier, no matter how

CHAPTER 1

Freedom and Creativity:
The Magic in Fly Design

I think of flies as pieces of art, as feelings first, as simple wonderings, as ideas next and finally as questions seeking solutions. The solutions are interesting but they are not the goal, only a part of the process of discovery.

The feeling always comes first. It may be sparked by the flick of a baitfish next to a rock or the sight of a seagull or tern or heron turning in mid-flight and landing. The feeling may trigger a memory from my boyhood or a story I have heard. It comes somehow and I am glad when it does. It opens me to creativity and I welcome and savor this. Sometimes I hold the feeling back, not allowing it to focus just yet. I let it grow in a hidden way waiting for it to unconsciously develop and burst forth and bud and perhaps bloom. I like this feeling of holding back and waiting for the right time. When it does come it holds many gifts.

I know the fly, the fish, the presentation, the color, the colors, the water, the quality of light and I know what it is I am looking for and I know how to form it and fish it and all of this comes in a flash without words. Then as I follow the feeling, the words come.

The materials are first reached for and then named and shaped and as I look at the fly, perhaps I will see another dimension to it or several, and I play with the theme. It may grow to be a fly that resonates with the insight that formed it from my feeling, or it may not. When I fish it, the fish themselves will answer the question. The worth of the fly is only that to me, and I leave it behind and move on to the next question. This, to me, is the essence of fly design.

If the idea of the fly holds and I can feel the adventure of discovering something, then I will try to refine it to its most simple form. The essence, or the idea, of the fly is much more important to me as the source or root of an expression or question than a single taxonomic image could ever be. A fly should work even as a non-exact or non-taxidermic reproduction because it has to imply more than what a light-reflective image can reproduce. It has to embody ordinariness, dimensionality, translucency, harmony, being and be dynamically balanced and integrated with the natural energies it is a part of.

This has been my observational and practical experience when tying flies to fish with. It is true for me. And yet, I know that this view is true in some form for all fly fishermen who tie flies for fishing even those who hold to the interpretations passed down within tradition and also for those who try to mimic nature through exact visual duplication. I know that they are attempting to portray the elusive look of life within the creature and they often do.

To capture the look of life through exact imitation is a perfectly reasonable approach to take, and when the definition of "exact imitation" is expanded to include the unknown and unexplored possibilities of that which any definition can never fully contain, then the probable and practical solutions become limitless. The imposed boundaries of fixed definition have no place in creative exploration. The boundary of a bent pin with a feather fastened to it had to be crossed before the Jock Scott could be imagined.

I seek the essential core first. Then, because I have an understanding of what idea is basic to the fly, I can add form and detail to it rather than starting with the focus on detail and a blind faith that the fly will contain that essential spark of life I seek. Sometimes the essence of a fly may be only a touch of color, perhaps orange with a touch of blue flash. That's it. A detail that is also the core. What can you do with something as vague as that? A great deal.

One dark and stormy night, while fishing a beach on Martha's Vineyard, I saw what felt to me like a touch of orange and a blue flash in the water and I became intrigued. I looked to where I had noticed it in the water and turned on my flashlight. There was a swarm of squid milling in the shallow water.

Later, I tied some flies with the orange and blue color note. I shaped them and built them from the idea of orange and blue flash at night equals squid to me, perhaps? The fly was the question and eventually with a little tweaking, it was answered by the fish with a yes. Is this fly the only question the fish say yes to? No! So I continue to find more questions. I choose to view it this way because it allows me the freedom to not have answers to depend on—only more and more questions. This attitude prevents me from becoming stale and rigid in my opinions and becoming fixed into a routine that excludes new ways of seeing familiar phenomena. It keeps me continuously fluid and always seeking what I have overlooked before.

Flies are beautiful objects. Paintings are beautiful objects. There is an energy within the Mona Lisa that cannot be captured by a paint-by-number reproduction even if Leonardo himself did it according to the directions. The energies used to form them are of different orders, the same is true with flies.

When I see photographs laid out in magazines and books of fly boxes neatly arranged with rows of patterns each exactly the same, I wonder why? They do look nice on a page, perhaps that's why. It is graphic design and it is sensitive to the pictorial and collectable beauty of fly patterns. There is much more to fishing with flies than the beauty and collectability of the patterns. The flies that are tied by fishermen are tied one at a time and they are all different. The pattern may be generic but the individual fly never is. Some flies are tied in such a way that they catch fish better than others. This is also a part of good fly design, creating each fly with an awareness of how the particular materials used interact with each other and how to form and balance them so they not only match a recipe but swim and move with the illusion of a living presence. Flies that are tied with this goal in mind are meaningful to the fishermen who tie and use them.

Allow yourself to tie flies from your feelings and show them to the fish. After all, that is how flies were made in the first place. Let the fish judge your flies. They are the connoisseurs of fly design and their verdict is the only one that counts.

Fly tying tradition is in a sense precious and it is to be respected. Respect is a very large word. It can be used as a doorway to knowledge and freedom or it can be interpreted as a binding to opinion and structure. Respect your own curiosity and explore from it. That is respecting and using the lore of the past. Knowing someone's work is important and, of course, this knowing, in and of itself, influences what it touches. Still, there are many Madonna and Child paintings and all are unique. Feelings are the fuel with which we create, and feelings, no matter how they come, belong to the one who feels them.

Honoring tradition does create and add a certain value to whatever a man does. To fashion a fly from tradition is an honorable practice. A tradition is a storehouse of knowledge that is available for exploration. Familiarity with a tradition can be empowering and yet, when this expertise is imposed to define correctness it diminishes into opinion. There are many opinions and there always will be room for many more. Hopefully there never will be a final word.

It is important to remember the root of fly tying. It is not to seek glory or identity from our fellow men but simply to tie flies as an expression of our feelings and ideas and to use them to catch fish. It is equally as important to honor the tradition of sharing with others what we have discovered and to humbly accept the fact that it is because of this spirit of sharing that we have come to know most of what we take for granted as fundamental in fly tying.

Once upon a time, there was no Lefty's Deceiver nor was there an idea of one but there was a feeling and a fellow who found it and held it and reached for the materials and named them and shaped them. Then he shared with others what he had found. The rest of the story is called tradition. It has no final page. There is no deadline for submittals.

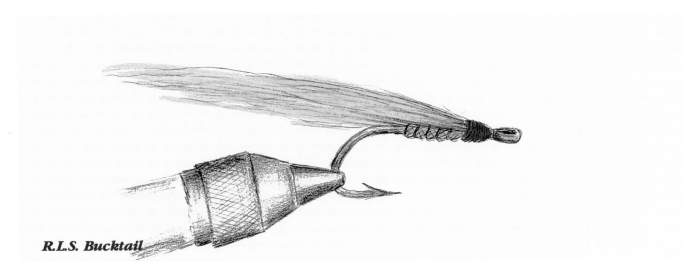

R.L.S. Bucktail

Tying Instructions for R.L.S. Bucktails

The simplest fly to tie that looks like a real fly is a hairwing. It has a body and a wing and the body is optional. To tie it you need some thread and a hook and a little bit of hair and something to wind on the shank of the hook for a body.

That really is all there is to it and of course you can add this and that and make it as complicated as you wish. I hope you do.

⑥

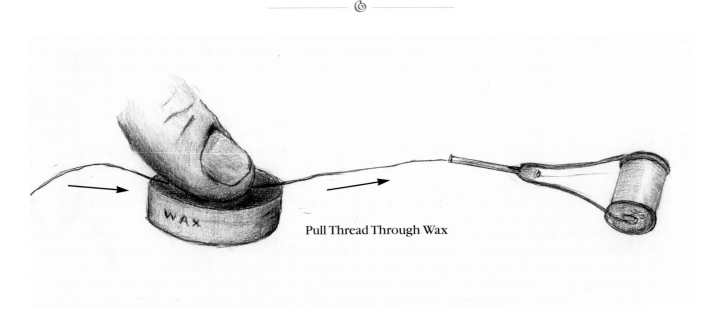

Pull Thread Through Wax

The thread you use should be of high quality and strong enough to bind and fasten the materials you are going to use to tie your fly. Coarse materials need strong thread and fine materials can be fastened with fine thread. Slippery thread slips and loosens over time unless you do something mechanically to compensate for this tendency. If you do not do something your flies will disintegrate quickly.

I like to wax my thread for tying. I use a mix of linseed oil and beeswax. Melt the beeswax and add a little linseed oil to it then let it cool. This mix is very tacky. I find that the tackiness of the wax helps my flies hold together by keeping the materials fixed in place. Another benefit to using wax is that it eliminates the need to use head cement. I complete my flies by tying three whip-finishes of four turns each. I have been finishing flies this way for many years. I find that it saves time by eliminating the tedious step of waiting for the paint to dry and re-coating it. My flies don't come apart very often.

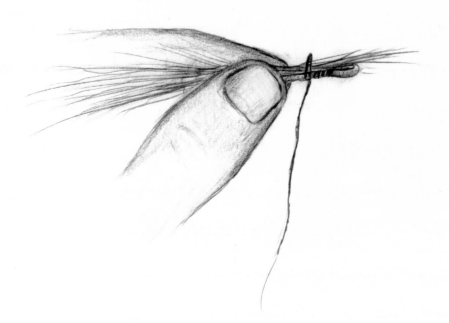

It is not hard to tie flies without a vise, you simply hold the hook in various ways and position the materials with the fingers that are holding the hook. The trick is to tie off each section of the fly as you complete it with a half hitch or two. It is a simple and easy process once you try it and it is much easier to do than threading a needle. I use a vise but I don't have to and neither do you. A good travel vise that you will never forget at home is your fingers.

❧

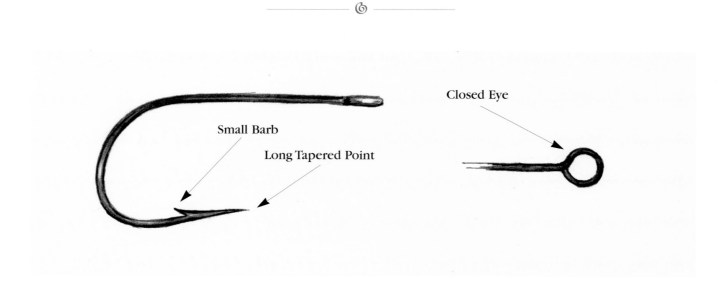

There are many hooks you can tie flies on. Some are very expensive and some are not. The price of a hook is unimportant and it is not the measure you should use to decide what hook to use.

The hook must be functional and trustworthy. It must be strong and extremely sharp. If it has a barb it must be well made and not too large. The point of the hook should be smooth and have a gentle taper so that it penetrates the fish's mouth with a minimum of resistance. The eye should be closed so that the leader will not slip into the space where the eye meets the shank and fall out. It is good practice to inspect every hook you use and be aware of its peculiarities before tying a fly on it.

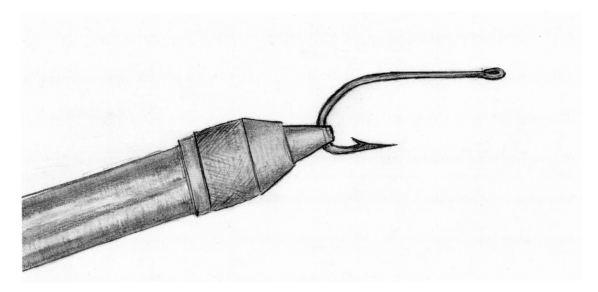

I find that the placement of the hook in the vise is an important step. The shank of the hook should be horizontal, not tipped up or down but perfectly flat. This is a step that is fundamental to the proper placement of materials but often overlooked by many beginning fly tiers. It is a structural squaring off similar to building a house on a firm and level foundation. It eliminates the visual distortion that occurs whenever something is perceived that is not quite level.

———————— ⑥ ————————

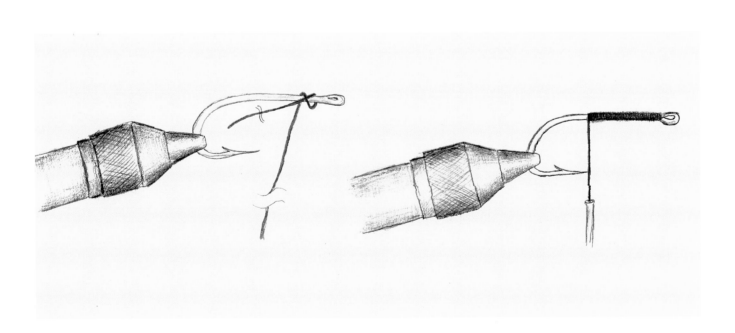

Secure the thread to the hook by overlapping and binding the end against the shank.

Wind the thread back toward the bend of the hook until it reaches a point directly above the point of the hook. This gives your fly a firm foundation that will help the materials to resist spinning or turning on the shank. It also exercises, develops and enhances the small motor control or manual dexterity that is needed for tying flies with graceful movement.

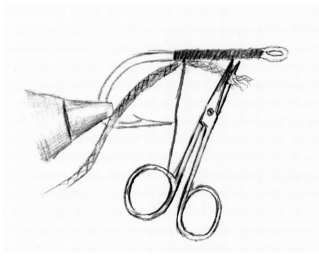

Bind the body material on the bottom of the hook shank. Wind the thread back up the shank, securing tag end to the bottom of the shank.

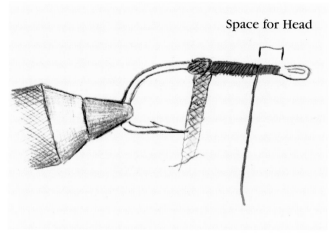

Space for Head

Wind the body material forward.

For this fly we will use a braided Mylar body material and wrap it forward, overlapping the previous turn by half the width of the braid to the point where the thread is hanging down and tie it off on the bottom of the shank.

This method ensures a solid-looking body with no gaps in the body of the fly.

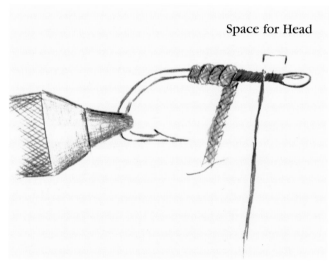

Space for Head

Overlap the previous turn by half the width of the body material.

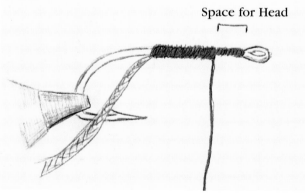

Space for Head

Finish winding leaving room for tying the wing and finishing the head.

Once the thread is wound on the shank to your satisfaction you can begin to tie on the material for the body. I find that it is best to bind the body material to the bottom of the hook shank directly above the point of the hook and wind the thread back up the shank, securing the tag end with the thread and forming a smooth underbody in the process. Remember to leave enough room to tie in the wing and the head comfortably. The distance between the hook point and barb on most hooks is just about the right amount of space to leave for the head.

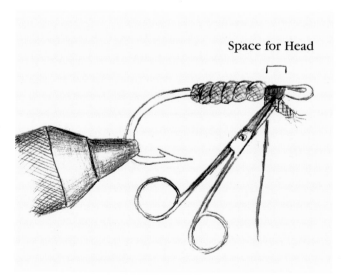

Space for Head

Tie off on the bottom of the hook shank.

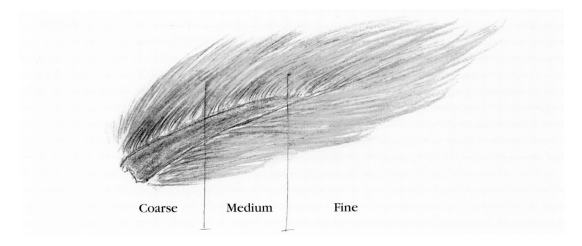

Coarse   **Medium**   **Fine**

Hair

The type of hair we use in tying a fly should be chosen because of how it will act in the water. Many fly tiers choose a hair simply because of the color or perhaps the pattern they are tying calls for a certain type of hair and they wish to follow directions. There is nothing wrong with this approach and in fact it is the only way to learn how to tie complicated patterns, nonetheless it will not guarantee that a particular fly will catch fish even though it is exact as to the materials used. Fly tying is not that simple. Certain flies catch fish better than others because they have the look of life within them. To tie flies that catch fish well we have to look at the hair we are going to use when tying a fly and evaluate it according to what we want that hair to do for us once it is tied into our fly. If the hair is soft it will move, if it is stiff it won't, simple enough, but soft is not better than stiff nor is stiff better

than soft. There will be times when stiff will be our choice for a variety of reasons and other times when soft will be the answer we need.

When tying a simple hairwing, first the hair must be chosen and then prepared for tying. There are many different types of hair and they all have unique characteristics. For this fly we will use bucktail hair.

Bucktail hair is not all the same. Some is fine and some is coarse. Each deer tail is different. When you choose a tail to tie flies with the hair that grew on that particular tail will determine the appearance of your fly. Coarse hair is rigid and hollow. Fine hair is soft and solid. A fly tied with coarse hair will be stiff and have a tendency to float or ride high in the water, whereas a fly tied with fine, solid hair will be supple when wet and will have neutral buoyancy.

🚦

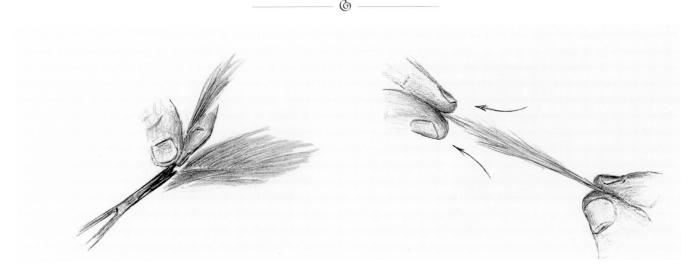

The first step in preparing bucktail hair for tying is to choose the section of hair to cut from the tail and then to remove the short hairs which bulk up the wing and add nothing to the movement and appearance of the fly. Hold the longest fine tips of the hair between the index finger

and the thumb, then grasp the butt or cut ends with the fingers of the other hand and gently pull the tips of the hair with the index finger and thumb until the long fibers are removed from the whole section. Repeat this until all the long hairs are separated from the bunch.

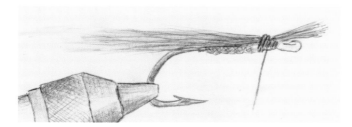

Long

Medium

Short

Separate the long hairs into three sections of different lengths, one with the longest hair, another with the shortest and a third with the medium.

Take the section of short hairs and count out thirty hairs and tie these on the top of the hook with two gentle turns of thread. Then manipulate these hairs with your fingers and spread them evenly on the top of the hook and to a point one third down both sides of the body, play with this until it looks good to you.

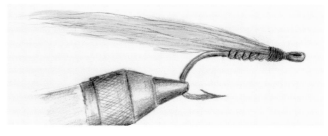

Next, wind another turn of thread with firmness between the two gentle turns and the eye of the hook to hold the hairs in place (you can use several turns to do this). The reason you secure the hair between the gentle wraps and the eye is simple, if you wrap the thread firmly below the gentle wraps the hair will flare up and out in all directions like a dandelion seed, the placement of the gentle wraps behind the firm ones hold the hair parallel to the hook shank. Cut the ends of the hairs (angled back neatly) with your scissors between the last turn of thread and the eye of the hook.

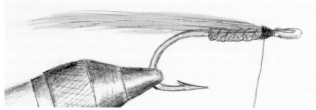

Take the medium hairs and count out twenty-five, repeat the steps, spreading and rolling the hair down to the same point on the side of the body. This will add length and symmetry to the wing without adding bulk. Cut the butt ends of the hair with careful attention to the end result.

The last step in tying the hairwing is to take the longest hair and count out twenty-two hairs, place them on top of the shank and repeat the process. Trim the ends of the hair again and even them up to form a smooth foundation for a neat head. Wind the thread mindfully, smoothing the head as you go by placing the thread in any indentations you see and finish with three whip-finishes or several half-hitches and head cement. Whip-finish.

Counting out hairs may seem like an unnecessary complication when tying flies and for many tiers it is. It enables those tiers who do use this step the ability to create and recreate with surety endless controlled style and color variations within the flies they tie. It facilitates the act of blending and matching subtle and pronounced variations in the color of all baitfish and crustaceans. It is simply a tool.

The steps that went into tying the basic hairwing streamer are fundamental steps that are used in many fly patterns. As you continue to tie you will develop your own style of tying and your flies will reflect your predilections. They will have personality and other tiers will be able to recognize them as yours with just a glance.

Tying a Whip-Finish

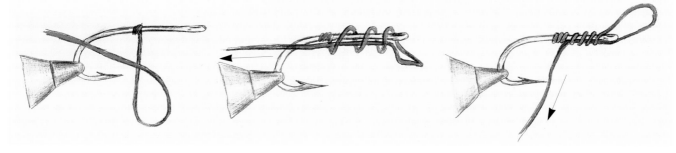

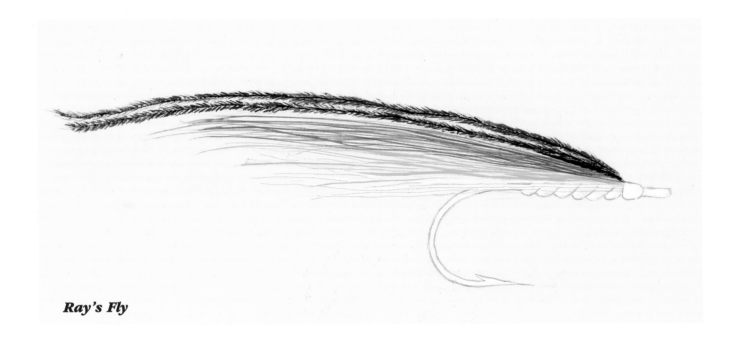

Ray's Fly

CHAPTER 2

R.L.S. Bucktails:
Ray's Fly

Afly is an idea. Some flies are created with the purpose of addressing and solving an angling problem and others are fashioned simply as expressions of the pure joy of speculative fly tying. I know a fly that fits into both of these categories. It is Ray's Fly.

It was late October many years ago, Geno Rapa and I had been fishing nights at "The Towers" in Narragansett, R.I. for a month. The fish had been cooperative but on this night they were being difficult. Fish were rising everywhere. They were popping and slashing in pursuit of silversides. We made cast after cast but they all came back empty. We tried poppers. We tried streamers. I even tried rubber wiggly things, but to no avail. Then Geno yelled, "Fish on!" Five more followed and number six took Geno's fly away. That was it. We didn't catch another fish for the rest of the night.

"What fly was that, Geno?" I asked later when we were in the parking lot. "Some kind of a silverside fly, I think. It was white and yellow and green and it had a black back and I don't have any more," he said in one breath. I began to rummage through my fly boxes looking for a fly that resembled his description. I finally found one, held it up for him to see and asked, "How about this?" He looked at it, looked up at me and said, "Kind of, only different."

The fly I had shown him had all the right colors, was the right size, but I had tied down the wing with a loose mono loop so it would not foul on the cast. I pulled the wing out from under the binding, held it out for him to see again and asked, "What about now?" "That's it. Yup, that's it," he answered.

Over the winter, I forgot all about that fly. The following spring, in late April, I was reminded of it again. Ray Bondorew and I were fishing the flood tide at Colt State Park in Bristol, R.I. The stripers were there and hitting well. Ray was fishing on one side of the river and was catching a lot of nice fish. I was on the other side and had fish in front of me but I could not hold on to them. My hooks were sharp. I was getting solid takes but I could not keep them on. I dropped eight fish in a row and finally landed one. I walked across the bridge and told Ray I was giving up. "What fly are you using?" I asked. There, in the light from my headlamp was a white, yellow and olive fly with a peacock herl topping. Some rainbow Krystal Flash and pearl Flashabou were mixed into the wing. The fly was about two and one half inches long tied on a number one hook. The body had been tied with silver Mylar yarn but it was gone, "They eat the bodies right off these flies, but it doesn't seem to bother them too much," Ray said with a smile.

That night I tied up ten of them and the following night found me back at Colt State Park fishing where Ray had been fishing the night before. The fish did not disappoint me. They took well and I had no trouble holding on to them. They did not hit Ray's fly—they ate it!

Ray originally tied the fly for fishing in the surf at a place called the "Clumps" at the mouth of the Narrow River in Narragansett, R.I. He was unsure if it would be productive because of its small size, but on his first cast to a pocket of white water he had success. Since that day Ray's Fly has become one of the most dependable striper flies ever designed. I am sure that many people have tied flies similar to Ray's Fly, but to those of us who know him this fly is Ray's. He had an idea, recognized its potential, worked it out and then shared it with everyone.

One evening too many years ago, I was fishing with Ray's Fly at the Bristol Narrows in Rhode Island. As I pulled my fly to the surface in preparation for another cast, I noticed a school of silversides swimming toward me. Their leader was swimming across a tide rip and moving steadily shoreward through the current. The school followed and was tightly formed around him. When I picked my fly out of the water the school scattered. Their leader was Ray's Fly. I guess that says it all.

Tying Instructions for Ray's Fly

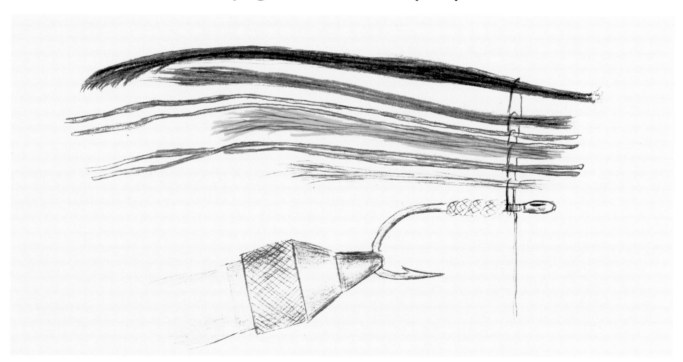

The first fly we will tie is the Ray's Fly. It is simple to tie and it is one of the best-producing flies ever created. It imitates the silverside and many other baitfish that are of the same coloration.

There are many variations of this fly. They all work. It is often tied with several hairs of blue bucktail mixed into the underwing and works equally well with different colors of Krystal Flash and is also tied with silver, gold, blue or green Flashabou mixed into the wing. Red works too.

Hook: 253 NA, 1X short, Eagle Claw, 2 through 3/0.
Thread: White.
Tail: None.
Body: Silver Mylar braid.
Wing: Bucktail; first white, 1 1/2 times the length of the hook, followed by two strips of pearl or silver Flashabou, next, yellow bucktail 1 3/4 times the length of the hook, then olive bucktail 2 times the length of the hook.
Topping: Seven strands of peacock herl tied as long or longer than the wing.
Eyes: Optional.

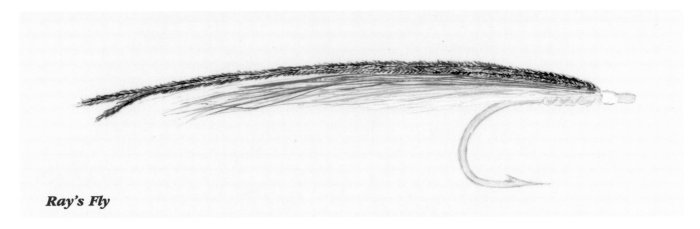

Ray's Fly

Ray's Fly is tied the same way as a basic hairwing but with the addition of three steps:
1. Three color changes in the wing.
2. Flashabou inserted within the wing.
3. Peacock herl topping over the wing.

Hook: Begin this fly by placing the hook in the vise correctly (horizontally) then tie on the white thread and wind it back toward the bend of the hook until it is located directly above the eye of the hook point.

Body: Using the point of the hook as a reference mark will enable you to recreate the "look of the fly," over and over again. Tie in the braid on the bottom of the shank, wind the thread forward to the place you want the body to end, (distance between the point and the barb) then wind the braid forward overlapping each turn by half. Tie off the braid on the bottom of the shank and cut off the end.

Wing: Bucktail, white, 1 1/2 length of hook, two strips of Flashabou, yellow bucktail, 1 3/4 the length of hook, olive bucktail two times the length of the hook.

Prepare the bucktail for tying by removing the short hairs from each color. Then separate the colors into three sections of different lengths: olive, the longest, white, the shortest and yellow for the medium.

Take the section of white hairs and count out approximately thirty hairs and tie these on the top of the hook shank with two gentle turns of thread. Then spread these hairs evenly across the top and one third down the sides of the body one and one-half times the length of the hook. Fix these hairs in position with several turns of thread positioned between the initial two gentle turns of thread and the eye of the hook. Cut the ends of the hairs (angled back neatly) with your scissors between the thread and the eye of the hook.

Place the two strips of Flashabou directly on top of the wing, extend them one inch beyond the tips of the hair then fasten and cut off. Take the yellow hairs, count out another thirty and repeat the tying steps, spreading and rolling the hair down to the same point on the side of the body. Optional step: place two more strips of Flashabou of a different color (blue, red, gold, green) on top of the yellow hair, the same length as the first then fasten and cut off.

Take between twenty and twenty-five of the olive hairs, tie them on top and roll them halfway down to the point where the yellow hairs were fastened.

Take seven strands of untrimmed peacock herl, wet them, and hold them horizontally between your finger and thumb. You will see the natural curve they take, place the strands on top of the olive with the curve side down and leave them 1/2 inch longer than the length of the bucktail, then tie and clip the waste ends off.

Trim the butt ends of the hair again and even them up to form a smooth foundation for a neat head. Wind the thread carefully, smoothing and building the head by filling in any indentations you see and finish the fly with personally waxed thread and three whip-finishes of four turns each or several half-hitches and head cement.

⑥

Tying Instructions for Little Sueshe

The next fly is called Little Sueshe. It is similar in construction to the first two except for the colors in the wing. We will use a wing made by blending several different colors of bucktail together to create a visual vibrancy that is impossible to duplicate with a monochromatic dye.

This way of mixing colors into the wing is very helpful and satisfying to learn and do. It will enable you to create an infinite number of interesting color variations in any fly by simply adding hues to the base color by counting the number of strands (hairs) of color and blending them in. It is also

R.L.S. Little Sueshe

helpful for creating color accents to the side of any fly with just a few colored hairs tied in as cheeks or shoulders.

Hook: 253 NA, 1X short, Eagle Claw, 2 through 3/0.
Tail: None.
Body: Silver or pearl Mylar braid.
Wing: Bucktail; white, yellow, pink, light blue, apple green, orange, violet, red, olive, medium blue and fluorescent yellow. Take 15 hairs of white 1 1/2 times the length of the hook, place them on top of the hook and roll them 1/3 down the side of the body, Then take 3 hairs of yellow, pink, light blue and apple green, mix them together by holding the tips and restacking them until they are blended together.

Place and tie these blended hairs on top of the white then tie in two strips of silver or pearl Flashabou on top, leaving the ends one inch longer than the wing.

Next, take 10 hairs of yellow bucktail 1 3/4 the length of the hook and mix 3 hairs of orange, fluorescent yellow, pink, light blue, violet and apple green into a single blended wing by repeating the stacking procedure. Tie this bunch of hair on top of the first bunch and roll it 1/3 down the side of the hook.

Blend together 5 hairs of olive bucktail 2 times the length of the hook with 5 hairs of violet, 5 of light blue, 3 of fluorescent yellow, 3 of orange and 3 of medium blue.

Topping: Seven strands of wetted peacock herl, curve side down, tied 1/2 inch longer than the wing.
Eyes: Jungle cock.

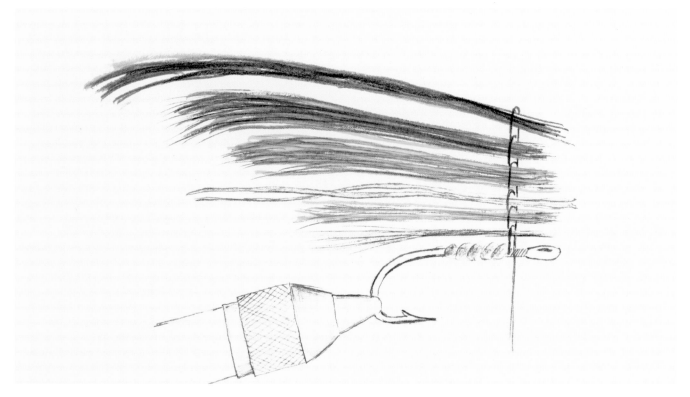

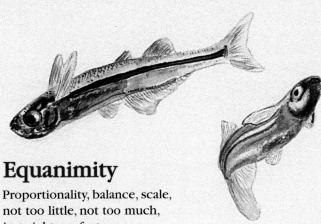

Equanimity

Proportionality, balance, scale,
not too little, not too much,
just right, perfect,
trying to be in harmony
with the laws of nature,
that's what it's all about.
Tying flies falls
into this equation.
Flies that are tied
with the harmony of nature
in mind are different
than flies tied without a thought
as to how they fit in with the way
things appear and act in nature.

Baitfish, and for that matter
all organisms that swim in water,
are in a state of equanimity, of rest.
Even those which
are injured and struggling
do so of their own volition
and when they stop struggling
are cradled and carried
by the water they are in.
The water they are in
does not move around them
unless they swim.
They are carried
along by current
and do not move
except by their own power.
Baitfish swim and they rest,
in either case they are
carried along by current.
Flies that imitate baitfish
should have
both of these characteristics
incorporated in their design.
They should look alive
when they are in motion
and they should also look alive
while at rest.
To accomplish this mix
takes real attention when tying
but the rewards while fishing
are extraordinary.

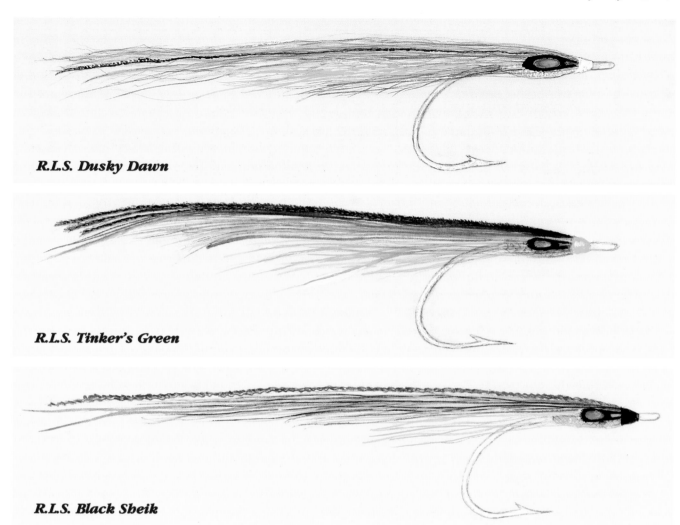

R.L.S. Dusky Dawn

R.L.S. Tinker's Green

R.L.S. Black Sheik

R.L.S. Dusky Dawn
Length: Tiny to large, 3/4 to 6 inches.
Hook: 253NA, 1X short, Eagle Claw, (all sizes).
Thread: White or yellow.
Tail: None.
Body: Gold or pearl Mylar braid.
Wing: Bucktail, 15 hairs of beige 1 1/2 times hook length under 20 hairs of yellow 2 times hook length, under 2 gold strips of Flashabou one inch longer than wing, under 2 pieces of peacock herl as long as the Mylar, under 10 hairs of light blue mixed with 10 hairs of light gray 3 times the length of the hook.
Cheeks: 3 hairs of light violet and 2 hairs of orange tied in full length on both sides.
Topping: None.
Eyes: Jungle cock.

R.L.S. Tinker's Green
Length: Tiny to large.
Hook: 253NA, Eagle Claw, all sizes.
Thread: Yellow.
Tail: None.
Body: Gold Mylar braid.
Wing: Bucktail, 15 hairs honey or amber mixed with 5 yellow and 5 orange hairs 1 1/2 times length of hook under 2 strips of emerald green Flashabou, under 7 hairs of lavender, 7 hairs of apple green and 7 hairs of light gray mixed and blended 2 times the length of the hook, under 10 hairs of olive, 5 hairs of light blue and 5 hairs of lavender 2 1/2 times the length of the hook.
Topping: 4 hairs of emerald green bucktail mixed with 3 hairs of deep blue at least 1/2 inch longer than the wing, under seven pieces of peacock herl.
Eyes: Jungle cock.

R.L.S. Black Sheik
Length: Tiny to large.
Hook: 253NA, Eagle Claw, all sizes.
Thread: Black.
Tail: None.
Body: Gold Mylar braid.
Wing: Bucktail, 12 hairs yellow 1 1/2 times length of hook under 8 hairs light blue, 8 hairs fluorescent yellow, 5 hairs orange mixed, 2 times the length of the hook, under 2 strips of blue Flashabou one inch longer than the wing, under 12 hairs of black, 15 hairs of olive mixed, 3 times the length of the hook.
Topping: 4 strands of root beer Krystal Flash one inch longer than the wing.
Eyes: Jungle cock.

Baitfish

I am fascinated by the baitfish I see and how they
appear to me in different conditions. My attention is
not focused on why they appear the way they do, I just try to
imitate their appearance somehow. When the water is clear they
sparkle brightly. When it has a greenish cast they sparkle but with
a glow to it, a different look. When the water is yellow with sediment they
don't sparkle but have another completely different look. When the water is
gray on an overcast day they appear different yet again. I delight in seeing
this difference. To me, knowing why it happens is only a small part of seeing.
I like to try and tie flies that imitate the different looks of the same
baitfish in its various casts of color. I will never capture them all or perhaps
never get any one of them exactly right, but I find the act of trying to do
it very satisfying.
How would you do it if you wanted to? Imagine a
silverside or any baitfish you know well in its colors and its
sheen and then picture it through a greenish glow like green
sea water. Next, clear water and sunlight and dawn, dusk,
and gray sky, midday and clouds.
It is a wonderful way to start a collection
of flies that are very personal—and it is a good way to
engage your powers of observation and discipline.
This kind of looking is more than a glance.
It is seeing what is really there
rather than assuming the answer.
Flies tied with this connection to
conditions work so very well and are so
unique that it may be a little unnerving
to the stockpiling part of human nature.
Tying each fly as a single creation
is a wonderful exercise in becoming
a better fisherman, simply
because you learn
to use your own
sensitivity to nature
as your major
resource. You
learn because
you don't
depend on
anything
but your
own sense
of wonder.

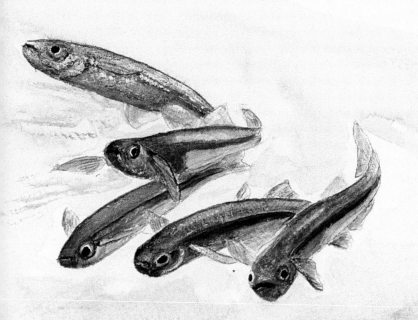

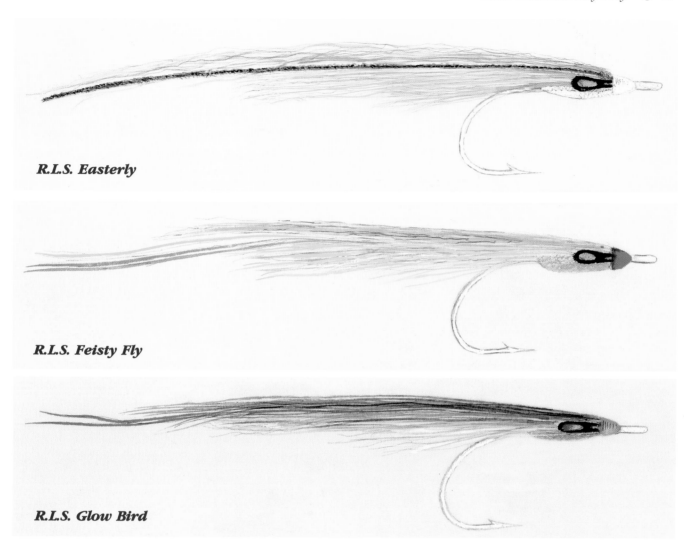

R.L.S. Easterly

R.L.S. Feisty Fly

R.L.S. Glow Bird

R.L.S. Easterly
Length: Tiny to large.
Hook: 253NA, Eagle Claw, all sizes.
Thread: White.
Tail: None.
Body: Silver or pearl Mylar braid.
Wing: Bucktail, 15 hairs of light gray 1 1/2 times the length of hook under 10 hairs of fluorescent yellow, 10 hairs of light gray mixed 2 1/2 times the length of the hook, under 4 strands of peacock herl, under 2 strips of silver Flashabou one inch longer than the wing, under 25 hairs of light gray 3 1/2 times the length of the hook.
Topping: None.
Eyes: Jungle cock.

R.L.S. Feisty Fly
Length: Tiny to large.
Hook: 253 NA, Eagle Claw
Thread: Orange.
Tail: None.
Body: Light. blue Mylar braid.
Wing: Bucktail, 15 hairs light ginger 1 1/2 times the length of the hook under 15 hairs light blue, 10 hairs fluorescent yellow mixed 2 1/2 times the length of the hook, under 2 strips of blue Flashabou, under 2 strips of emerald green Flashabou, under 2 strips (one each) of silver and gold Flashabou one inch longer than the wing, under 15 hairs of light gray, 10 hairs of light blue, 3 1/2 times the length of the hook, mixed.
Topping: None.
Eyes: Jungle cock.

R.L.S. Glow Bird
Length: Tiny to large.
Hook: 253 NA, Eagle Claw.
Tail: Thread: Pink.
Body: Pink Mylar braid.
Wing: Bucktail, 15 hairs of white, 8 hairs of pink 1 1/2 times the length of the hook mixed under 7 hairs of light violet, 4 hairs of yellow, 5 hairs of light blue, 5 hairs of silver doctor blue, 5 hairs of pink 2 1/2 times the length of the hook, mixed, under 2 strips of red Flashabou one inch longer than the wing, under 10 hairs of lavender, 4 hairs of fluorescent red 3 times the length of the hook, mixed, under 5 hairs of dark blue, 4 hairs of emerald green mixed, 3 1/2 times the length of the hook.
Topping: None.
Eyes: Jungle cock.

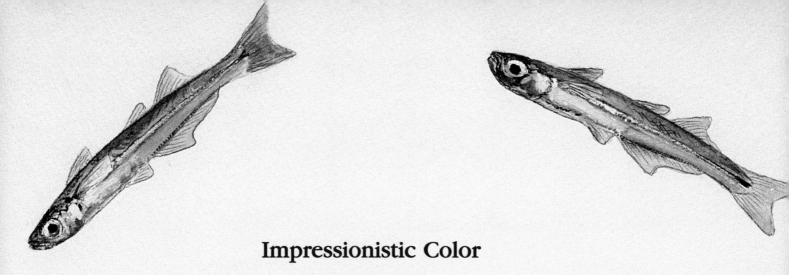

Impressionistic Color

Even simple patterns,
simple in execution if not in presence,
can be modified to suit any nuance endlessly.
Color alone can engage any fly
tier for years with its complexities.
Many people think of color as uniform,
like a painted wall, but in nature
color is never flat in appearance.
That is one reason why mixing
different colored hairs of bucktail
or other hair is so satisfying to the eye.

I use dyed hairs if I like the color and
mix them to suit my need or desire.
The effects are quite lifelike,
in fact they often appear to have a glow.
Colors have an effect upon each other to the eye.
They mix and form secondaries and tertiaries and so on and yet
they retain their original hue.
So there is this constant shifting in what the eye sees,
a type of movement from within the fly itself
of colors merging and forming other colors.
This effect is a wonderful addition to any fly.
If blue and yellow hairs are blended together
they form green, if red is added, it will create the
accidental effect of producing orange and purple
and the colors in-between.
These accidental effects are simply beautiful.

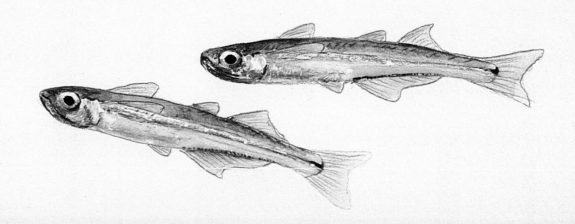

R.L.S. Stormy Sea

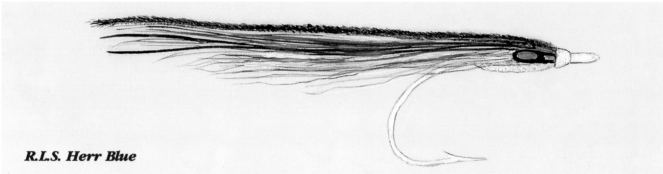

R.L.S. Herr Blue

R.L.S. Manitoo

R.L.S. Stormy Sea

Length: Tiny to large.
Hook: 253 NA, Eagle Claw.
Thread: Chartreuse.
Tail: None.
Body: Silver or pearl Mylar braid.
Wing: Bucktail, 10 hairs of light gray, 10 hairs of apple green 1 1/2 times the length of the hook, mixed, under 7 hairs of orange, 7 hairs of pale yellow, 7 hairs of silver doctor blue 2 1/2 times the length of the hook, mixed, under 2 strips of gold Flashabou, under 14 hairs of smoky green gray, 14 hairs of apple green 3 1/2 times the length of the hook, mixed.
Topping: None.
Eyes: Jungle cock.

R.L.S. Herr Blue

Length: Tiny to large.
Thread: White.
Hook: 253 NA, Eagle Claw.
Tail: None.
Body: Silver Mylar braid.
Wing: Bucktail, 15 hairs white, 5 hairs of ginger 1 1/2 times the length of the hook, mixed, under 8 hairs of violet 4 hairs of pink, 10 hairs of light blue 2 times the length of the hook, mixed, under 2 strips of silver Flashabou, under 2 strips of purple Flashabou, under 10 hairs of dark blue, 4 hairs of emerald green, 6 hairs of smoky blue gray, 4 hairs of orange 3 times the length of the hook, mixed.
Topping: 7 strands of peacock herl.
Eyes: Jungle cock.

R.L.S. Manitoo

Length: Tiny to large.
Hook: 253 NA, Eagle Claw.
Thread: Turquoise.
Tail: None.
Body: Silver Mylar braid.
Wing: Bucktail, 10 hairs of white, 5 hairs of ginger, 5 hairs of pink 1 1/2 times the length of the hook, mixed, under 5 hairs light orange, 10 hairs turquoise, 10 hairs of pale yellow 2 1/2 times the length of the hook, mixed, under 2 strips of light blue Flashabou under yellow, light gray, turquoise, 10 hairs each, 3 1/2 times the length of the hook, mixed.
Topping: None.
Eyes: Jungle cock.

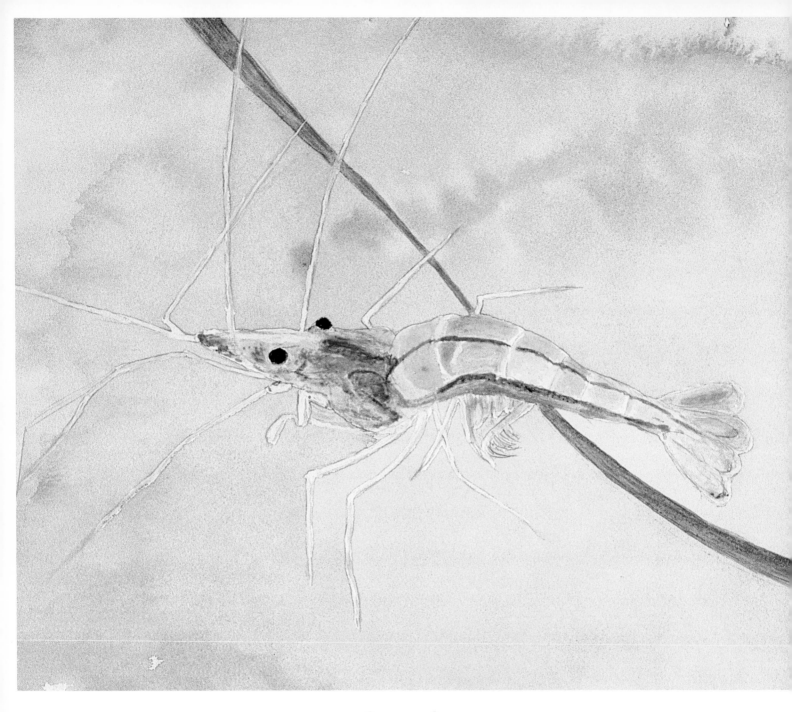

CHAPTER 3

Shrimp

It is the look of living grass shrimp that is important to fish. They do not see shrimp as we do, with our associations of shrimp as "cocktails" and in supermarket packages. Fish see them as they appear to them, a shape that is diffused by the light passing through. If we were to view the shrimp from their position we might say that it is transparent with a gray cast and it has life within it. If we were to change our physical location perhaps from a tidal river to a lagoon, we could notice that the shrimp may have color variations depending on the environment in which we found them. Some would appear greenish, some would have different casts of amber, others, a speckled salt and pepper with a light chartreuse glow. Some shrimp would be large and some very tiny. We would find that there is no standard look to a shrimp except that they are alive, have vibrancy within them and light passes through their bodies.

Grass shrimp mate at night in the spring on the dark of the moon. They mate at different times in different places, but in the tidal rivers that feed Narragansett Bay, the new moon in May is when the bulk of them rise to the surface film from the bottom and are carried along by the currents as darkness thickens.

Stripers that are feeding on these mating shrimp take positions in the current and hold on station to feed. They wait in the current and pick them off one at a time as the shrimp drift down over their stations. The rises are slightly different depending on the current flow through the striper's holding position. If the current is fast the fish makes a tight energetic boil accompanied by a loud popping sound, if the current is slow, the rise is gentle, followed by a tail wiggle, i.e., a classic head and tail rise.

Saltwater fly fishermen who do not know of this selective feeding by striped bass on grass shrimp are often stymied in their first attempts to catch these fish. What starts off as excitement about the good fortune of finding stripers feeding on the surface soon turns into the frustration of not being able to catch them at all and the confusion that comes with not knowing why.

Ordinarily, saltwater fly fishermen look at the fly patterns they use as the major reason they do or do not have success and overlook anything beyond this simple and easy explanation. Fly choice is important when fishing for stripers that are feeding in a fixed rhythm but what is more important is being aware of the rhythm and its measure and beat. Before the fly pattern can be judged to be incorrect, a good look at the stripers' feeding behavior and a dispassionate evaluation of the presentations that were used is in order.

Stripers often act in a way that mirrors the behavior of trout in a stream. This is simple to understand. The water is moving. The current is focusing the drifting food and the fish are holding and feeding on the food that is being brought to them by the current. They come to the surface to eat it and break the surface in some visible way. Their behavior is no different than trout because the same factors are present. The approach is to fish for them the way you would fish for trout that are feeding during a hatch.

The first order of business is to find out what they are feeding on. There are many ways to do this but only one that is a sure revealer of what is coming down the current. A fine mesh net, about a foot across, will tell you in short order what you need to know. The net will be most effective if you look at the current and place it where there is a focusing of the flow. You will soon find out what the stripers are feeding on, or at least you will have an idea of what is in the river at that time. Once you have an idea of the types of animals present in the water you can easily deduce an approach. The net will capture anything that is in the water. This is often a revelation as you will find shrimp, tiny fingerlings, swimming worms or anything else that is present and this cornucopia of life can be confusing when it is unexpected. These creatures are found swimming or floating in the surface currents of most tidal streams from the larger rivers to the tiny outflows that pass under roads through culverts. They are fed upon by stripers in all these flows.

If you find a school of stripers feeding in the evening at this time of the year they are often feeding on larger baitfish such as silversides and they can be caught fairly easily with streamer flies that approximate the size of the baitfish present. Once darkness comes, however, often the feeding pattern of the stripers changes.

As darkness covers the water, shrimp and other creatures come to the surface and the sheer numbers of them may cause the stripers to change their feeding pattern, and even though there are still as many silversides as there were earlier, the bass will begin to ignore them and start to refuse the streamer patterns. They will move their focus to the shrimp or some other prevalent species. This is often the undoing of a successful fishing trip. It is an ordinary scenario when fishing in tidal water in the spring but many fishermen do not realize it because there is no obvious change in the behavior of the bass and this masks or makes it seem as if there is no change in their feeding pattern.

The saltwater fly fisherman may or may not have awareness of these quirks in the feeding behavior of stripers. If he or she does, catching these fish is not a problem to them at all, rather, it is the type of fishing situation experienced fly fishermen welcome. It connects their fascination with learning and understanding more about the ocean and fish behavior to a new experience. It is essentially a part of the adventure of discovering the mysteries of saltwater fly fishing—the ocean equivalent of what is so appealing and fascinating within the traditions of trout fly fishing. Those saltwater fly fishermen who are not familiar with this root of fly fishing will either fail to catch these fish entirely or learn that much of what they have been taught about fly fishing and striper behavior could be a handicap and may have to be reviewed and re-evaluated in light of their actual personal experience.

Stripers in tidal water feed in a contained environment the same way that trout in a river feed. How their food is acting in relationship with that environment will determine how they will behave. There is no barrier to learning these striper secrets easily except for an unwillingness to patiently observe and begin to explore and see what nature is actually displaying right before us and then act in a way that will allow our efforts to be in intelligent harmony with it.

General Practitioner

General Practitioner Tying Instructions

The General Practitioner is a very old pattern that imitates a shrimp very well. It is made from natural materials fashioned with traditional techniques. It is fun to tie and experiment with.

Hook: 255NA, Eagle Claw.
Antennae: Hot orange bucktail.
Head: (Short feelers and mouth parts) fire orange hackle tip.
Eyes: Golden pheasant tippet feather with center cut out to form a vee shape and lacquered.
Carapace: Red golden pheasant breast feather.
Body: Hot orange wool.
Ribbing: Oval tinsel, gold.
Hackle: Hot orange, palmered over whole body.
Back: Red golden pheasant breast feather.
Tail: Red golden pheasant breast feather.

Golden pheasant tippet feather

Next lay the trimmed golden pheasant tippet on top of the hackle feather with the fibers pointed parallel to the bucktail fibers.

Golden pheasant breast feather

Then place the first golden pheasant breast feather on top to form the carapace: The feather is tied on flat like a little roof. Wind the material ends down the shank to form a uniform underbody and then wind the thread back to the starting point.

There are several ways to tie this fly, all are effective. Tying instructions: Tie in the bucktail fibers directly above the barb of the hook. They should flare slightly and be pointed down. Then tie in the hot orange hackle tip above the bucktail horizontally.

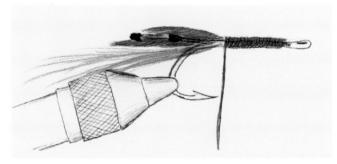

Pick a hot orange hackle with fibers one and one half the length of the gap of the hook and tie it in at the bottom of the shank. Next, tie in the gold oval tinsel at the bottom and then the hot orange wool. Wind the wool to the middle of the shank and tie off on the bottom of the shank then wind the ribbing to the same point with three turns and tie off at the bottom also. Do not cut off the ends but leave them long as they will be used for the front part of the body.

Next, palmer the hackle down with each turn

behind and touching the turns of oval tinsel, tie it off on the bottom and cut the remainder. Clip the hackle off the top of the hook and fasten the second golden pheasant breast feather as a flat roof above it.

Tie in another orange hackle and repeat these steps for the front part of the body. Top off the fly with the third breast feather make a neat head and whip-finish with four turns, three times.

In the patterns that follow the same tying steps are repeated, I will only list the materials for each fly.

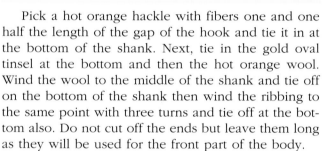

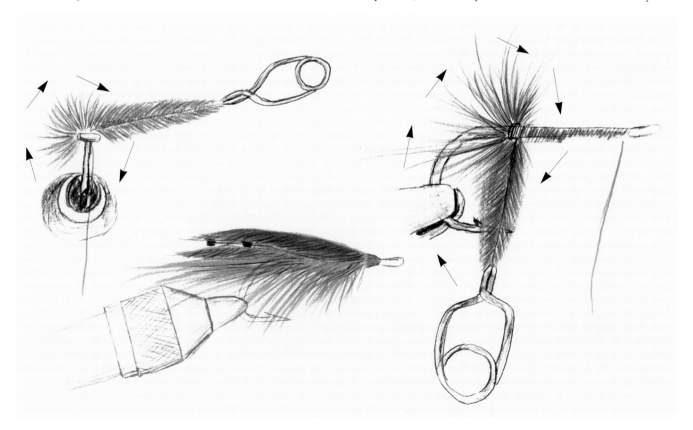

Note: The General Practitioner is a very effective clam worm imitation, often outfishing every other fly.

Shrimp

In the spring, on the New Moon, shrimp come to the surface
to mate. They are carried along by the currents and are preyed upon
by stripers and other game fish.

Stripers that are feeding on these mating shrimp hold in feeding stations.
They position themselves in the current and sip in the shrimp as they drift down
over their feeding station.

A floating line with a dead-drift presentation will catch these fish. The fly should be
high in the water, as close to the surface as possible. Greasing the leader and fly helps.
With the dead-drift presentation the fly should be cast above the rising fish and allowed
to float over the fish's position in the current. This maneuver can be executed either
upstream, cross-stream, downstream and every place in-between. You will have to tend
your line differently depending on what direction you choose.

If you choose to fish upstream you will have to gather in the line as the line and
the fly come down the current towards you. If you choose to fish cross-stream then
you will have to mend the line so that drag does not pull the fly out of the fish's
feeding lane. If you choose to fish downstream then you will have to have slack line
in hand and be prepared to feed this line into the drift to allow the fly to drift
over the fish naturally.

When fishing the downstream drift one has to learn how to hook fish
consistently. The fish do not aggressively pursue the fly and engulf it,
they simply rise and sip it in. The tightness of the line prevents the fly
from entering their mouth as a free-floating shrimp would and when
they close their mouth there is nothing in it. When the angler
attempts to set the hook after seeing the rise or after having felt
the bump of the fish's attempt to suck the shrimp in, there is
no fish there to hook. Often the angler concludes that
the fish has struck short but this is seldom the case,
the tension on the line is the force that prevents the
fish from completing the take. The secret is in
finding the balance of just enough slack in
the leader and just enough patience to
wait for the fish to turn down
with the fly securely
within its mouth.

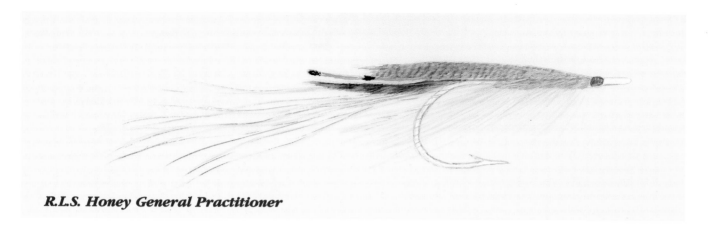

R.L.S. Honey General Practitioner

R.L.S. Bronze General Practitioner

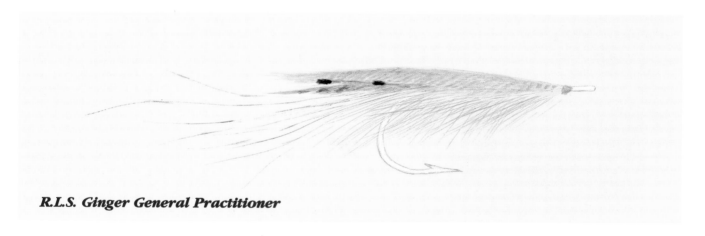

R.L.S. Ginger General Practitioner

R.L.S. Honey General Practitioner
Hook: 255NA, Eagle Claw.
Antennae: Gray fox.
Head: Cock-y-bondhu hackle tip.
Eyes: Golden pheasant tippet.
Body: Amber wool
Ribbing: Oval gold tinsel.
Hackle: Pale gray (watery dun) hackle.
Carapace: Lemon wood duck.
Back: Lemon wood duck.
Tail: Lemon wood duck.

R.L.S. Bronze General Practitioner
Hook: 255NA, Eagle Claw.
Antennae: Red fox.
Head: Cock-y-bondhu hackle tip.
Eyes: Golden pheasant tippet.
Body: Amber wool.
Ribbing: Gold oval tinsel.
Hackle: Cock-y-bondhu.
Carapace: Dyed bronze mallard (light).
Back: Same.
Tail: Same.

R.L.S. Ginger General Practitioner
Hook: 255NA, Eagle Claw.
Antennae: Gray fox.
Head: Cock-y-bondhu hackle tip.
Eyes: Golden pheasant tippet.
Body: Cream wool.
Ribbing: Gold oval.
Hackle: Ginger.
Carapace: Pintail.
Back: Same.
Tail: Same.

Acting

My dad showed me how to tie flies when I was very little.
I do not know how old I was but I remember the evening
every time I smell the scent of feathers and bucktail
with the pungency of moth balls.
It is a perfume, the scent of recollection.

Smells take us back so very fast to exact time and place
as if we were there in the now,
and perhaps we are there in essence, and who can deny it.

I can smell stripers sometimes.
I have followed my nose to find fish.
It is not hard to do at all, anyone can do it.
All that is required is to know
what you are smelling when you smell it.
It is that simple.
They smell like fish,
fish that some say
smell like melons or cucumbers.
I say yes, and that too
but they smell like stripers
and I don't have to wonder
what they smell like when I smell them.

I say, "Hey, I smell bass," and look upwind,
that is where they will be in the direction of the wind.
So simple really. No magic except for the magic of smell
and being present to your sensitivity
and believing in your knowing something real
with no corroborating certification.
"How did you catch those fish?" he asked.
"I smelled 'em first and then I caught 'em."
That's the only certification possible,
the corroboration of acting and having the experience.

We human beings have a lot of
talents and possibilities we already use,
and mysteriously we have others
that we are reluctant to be conscious of
and prefer to disregard and ignore.
Why?

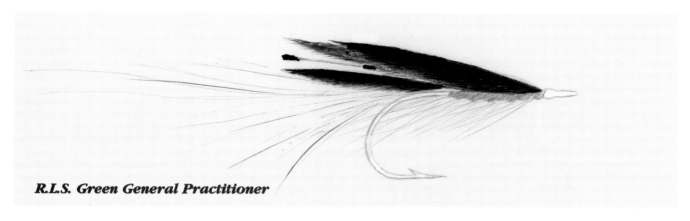

R.L.S. Green General Practitioner

R.L.S. Pink General Practitioner

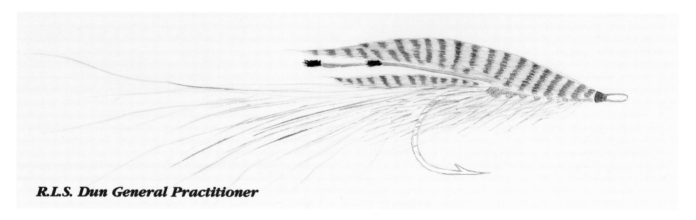

R.L.S. Dun General Practitioner

R.L.S. Green General Practitioner
Hook: 255NA, Eagle Claw.
Antennae: Turquoise and olive bucktail.
Head: Black feather from the neck of a golden pheasant.
Eyes: Golden pheasant tippet.
Body: Gold flat tinsel.
Ribbing: Gold oval tinsel.
Hackle: Pale green hackle.
Carapace: Guinea body feather dyed green.
Back: Same.
Tail: Metallic green turkey body feather.

R.L.S. Pink General Practitioner
Hook: 255NA, Eagle Claw.
Antennae: Amber bucktail.
Head: Claret hackle tip.
Eyes: Golden pheasant tippet.
Body: Pink wool.
Ribbing: Oval silver tinsel.
Hackle: Pale pink.
Carapace: Red golden pheasant breast feather.
Back: Same.
Tail: Same.

R.L.S. Dun General Practitioner
Hook: 255NA, Eagle Claw.
Antennae: Gray squirrel.
Head: Teal.
Eyes: Golden pheasant tippet.
Body: Silver flat tinsel.
Ribbing: Gold oval tinsel.
Hackle: Grizzly.
Carapace: Teal.
Back: Teal.
Tail: Teal.

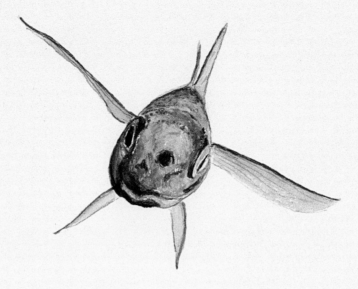

The
First
Impression

Within the first impression
you have of something is the perception of a feeling.
This is awareness.
Within the recognition of this feeling lie all the roots
to your second and third impressions.
They are not the same as the first.
When you hold nature in front of you,
it is easy to forget the essence
of that first inspiring impression
from which your ideas flow.
The feeling should be linked
to your first impression,
get it down and do not abandon it.
It is the germ from which great flies grow.

Hold to it the first time through,
if it dies it dies, there is no loss.
You gain from the experience
and then it's time to look again, anew.

And then perhaps, but only then,
the second glance.
The second is the new,
the beginning of the next round.
New ground, no fertilizer needed.
Run with the new, let it flow.
No detailing please.

R.L.S. Glo Bug Blue General Practitioner

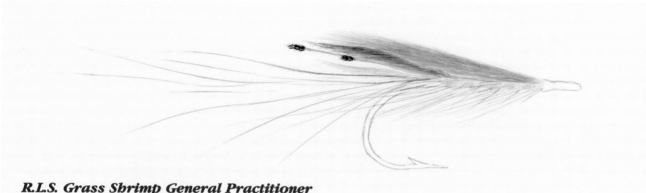

R.L.S. Grass Shrimp General Practitioner

R.L.S. Parrot Shrimp General Practitioner

R.L.S. Glo Bug Blue General Practitioner

Hook: 255NA, Eagle Claw.
Antennae: Violet and pink bucktail.
Head: Ring-necked pheasant rump feather.
Eyes: Golden pheasant tippet.
Body: Glo Bug Yarn, blue, left rough looking.
Carapace: R.N.P. rump feather.
Back: Same.
Tail: Same.

R.L.S. Grass Shrimp General Practitioner

Hook: 255NA, Eagle Claw.
Antennae: Olive bucktail.
Head: Chartreuse hackle tip.
Eyes: Golden pheasant tippet.
Body: Olive yellow floss.
Rib: Oval pearl tinsel.
Hackle: Light olive.
Carapace: Dark olive hackle tip.
Back: None.
Tail: Any soft, light olive hair.

R.L.S. Parrot Shrimp General Practitioner

Hook: 255NA, Eagle Claw., Eagle Claw.
Antennae: Blue and chartreuse bucktail.
Head: Fire orange hackle tip.
Eyes: Golden pheasant tippet.
Body: Chartreuse floss.
Rib: Gold oval tinsel.
Hackle: Golden yellow.
Carapace: Chartreuse hackle tip.
Back: None.
Tail: Ring-necked pheasant rump feather dyed chartreuse.

CHAPTER 4

A Stick and a String:

The Fly Rod as a Fly Rod

A Primer of Non-spinning Traditional Fly Fishing Presentation

"It is not how far you can cast that is the measure of your ability as a fisherman, it is how well you fish the cast you can make." My father taught me that when I was a boy. He gave me my first fly rod and gave me one casting lesson. He told me to pay attention to nature, and get as close as I could to the fish. It was good advice.

Fly fishing is unique in that, out of all the forms of angling, it alone elegantly and gracefully solved the problems of presenting weightless flies to fish that were focused on food that was brought to them by current.

The ocean is not a static stillwater environment. Tide is not just the rise and fall of water level, it is also the ebb and flow. A one-inch rise in tide entails the movement of enormous quantities of sea water from one place to another. This movement is a continous phenomena on the whole planet. Fish, whether they are on the flats in Florida or the Connecticut shoreline of Long Island Sound, move and feed in relation to this tidal movement. It is in this type of moving water environment that the fly rod's capacity for presentation shines. It has no peer for delivering flies in harmony with the dynamics of moving water. The secret of the fly rod's ability to perform this is the manipulation of the line.

Fly fishing is line handling. It is the line that allows the rod to flex and cast and carry the weightless fly to its destination. It is the line that floats or sinks and determines the depth where the fly will swim. It is the line that is acted upon by the force of current and it is the line that becomes the conduit that transmits this energy into drag. The term "drag" is an old fly fishing term that has nothing to do with the braking function of a modern fly reel. Line handling is the ability to harness this force through mending and use it to perform most of the sophisticated presentation techniques that are the backbone of traditional fly fishing.

Striped bass and other game fish can be caught with incredible consistency if one is willing to look into the nurturing relationship that current, no matter how slight or seemingly imperceptible it may be, has with feeding fish. Current is the underlying order that makes it possible to begin to understand the behavior of stripers and other predatory fish with any degree of certainty, however limited it may be. With this awareness, presentation, in all of its forms, becomes the most important skill a fly fisherman can develop. At that point of understanding, what becomes even more important than being able to cast a long line is the ability to handle that line with control once it is in the water.

Using traditional presentation techniques to catch fish that are holding in current to feed adds so much to saltwater fly fishing that it should be explored for the pure joy of discovery. Engaging the difficulties of proper presentation is perhaps the most wonderful part of fishing with a fly rod. The simplicity of casting a long line and stripping back a fly is a way of fishing with the fly rod but it bypasses the full scope that understanding and using traditional presentation techniques encompasses. Fly fishing has a long and rich heritage and much of this is about fishing with an awareness of the fundamental energies that are involved when fly fishing. To recognize and interact with them intelligently is to embrace fly fishing's unique methodology and to grow in awareness with understanding and appreciation of the roots and history of fly fishing's ancient link with moving water. Saltwater fly fishing is a part of that tradition. A true "new and exciting frontier" for saltwater fly fishing would be to embrace and explore the central and fundamental role that reading current, understanding drag and skillful presentation have always played in fly fishing. To understand these energies and use them artfully is the essential core of what it has always meant to be a knowledgeable and gifted fly fisherman.

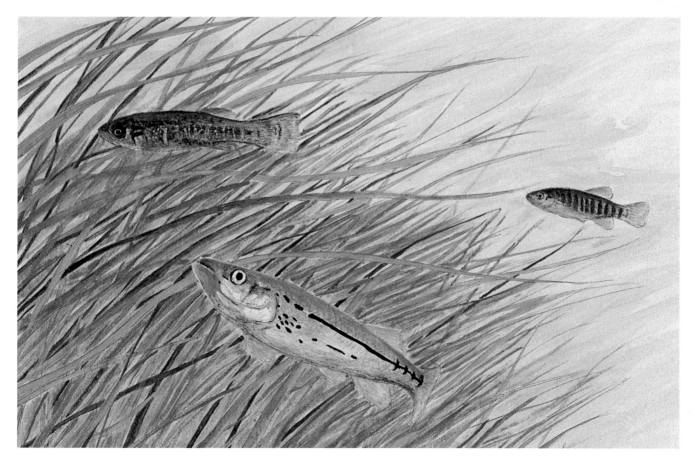

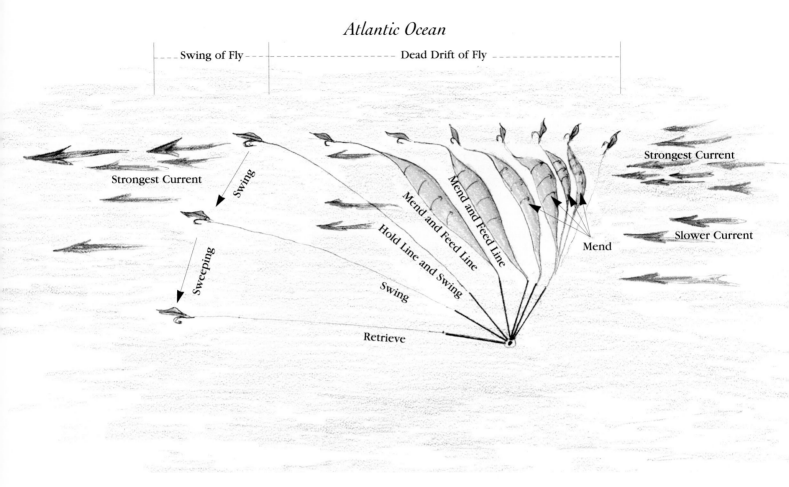

Dead-Drift or Drag-Free Float

(Dead-drift describes the energy of the presentation.)

Executed by mending upstream ending in wet-fly swing of sweeping swing.
Fly remains in one current seam until it crosses in its sweep at the end of drift.

The drag-free float or the dead drift is not a mysterious presentation. It is simply preventing drag from moving your fly sideways through the current. When done in its purest form the fly drifts in the flow as if it were not attached to your leader. This presentation is very effective when stripers are feeding on grass shrimp, clam worms, tiny fry or any other free-drifting organisms that are being carried along in the stream. There are many techniques one can use to accomplish this from standing directly upstream of where you wish your fly to drift and letting the line flow through your guides without resistance, to casting across the flow and then stacking the line upstream of your fly with a series of upstream mends. Mending is easily accomplished by pointing the rod toward the fly, tightening the line and picking it up off the water with a half roll in an upstream direction. The rod stays out in front of you throughout the entire motion and passes through an arc that can be visualized as a rainbow with one end where your fly is and the other end where you want the mend to land. With practice this movement becomes second nature and you will be able to shoot line into your mend and never move your fly.

When stripers are feeding on free-drifting organisms they can be as selective as any spring creek trout. Fly pattern can be the answer but if the fly is not presented correctly you will continue to have difficulty even with the correct pattern and size.

Deep-Drift, Long Leader and Weighted Fly
Cast is stopped in air to let fly sink on loose leader
then mended to allow it to sink free of "lift of current" through drag.

This presentation incorporates the dead drift and mending to give control over the depth a fly will fish. It can be accomplished with a long leader, split shot and a floating line or a sink-tip or a weighted fly. The fly is cast above where you think a fish is holding. The line is mended upstream to allow the fly to freely sink to the depth you wish it to be without the force of drag pulling it toward the surface. The fly should precede the leader and line as it moves downstream towards the position you wish to fish. When it reaches that point tighten the line and swim the fly with a leading swing if possible or hold the line and simply let the current swing the fly across with a wet-fly swing. If you can mend well and can keep your fly drifting freely on an almost tight line then this technique can be used with great effectiveness because you will be able to control the depth of your fly with your mends and be able to detect the fish simply stopping the fly as it moves downstream.

* Note it is not the weight of the rod
or the strength of the rod that is tiring,
it is the balance—the balance must be in the hand not above it.

Cape Cod Bay

*Fly is led and dropped downstream, past rock (leading swing)
next it is swept across current in sweeping swing or wet-fly swing.*

Sweeping Swing or Wet-Fly Swing

(Sweeping swing describes the energy of the presentation)
Sweeps fly across the current in an arc under tension
like a sail boat tacking into the wind.
Fish see the tail of the fly first.

This presentation swims the fly across the current in a sweeping motion. It is the simplest of all the line-handling presentations and can be used with sinking lines effectively in certain areas where the current will keep the line straight to the fly throughout the swing. It is accomplished by casting down and across the current and letting the current swing the line toward the bank you are standing on. This is a good technique for searching or sweeping the water below you for active fish. The classic approach to this technique is to make a short cast and fish out the swing then add three feet to each successive cast until you have reached your comfortable casting limit. At that point you take a step downstream between casts covering all the water below you by sweeping the fly across the currents one step at a time. It is a reasonable approach to fishing blind and it is a very effective way to deliver your fly to a fish that is rising downstream from your position. It is a salmon technique that works well on stripers and has the unique quality of moving your fly through every section of downstream water within your casting range systematically.

Long Island Sound

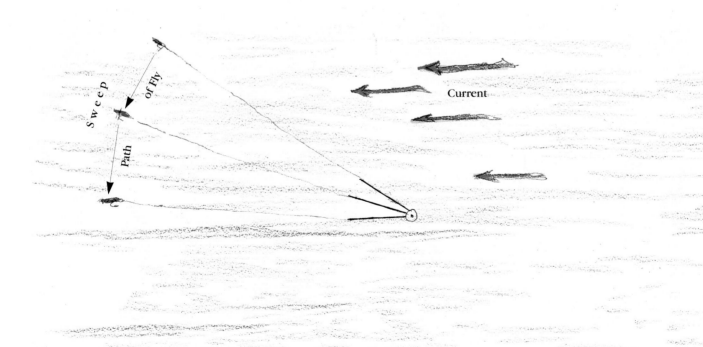

Caribbean Sea

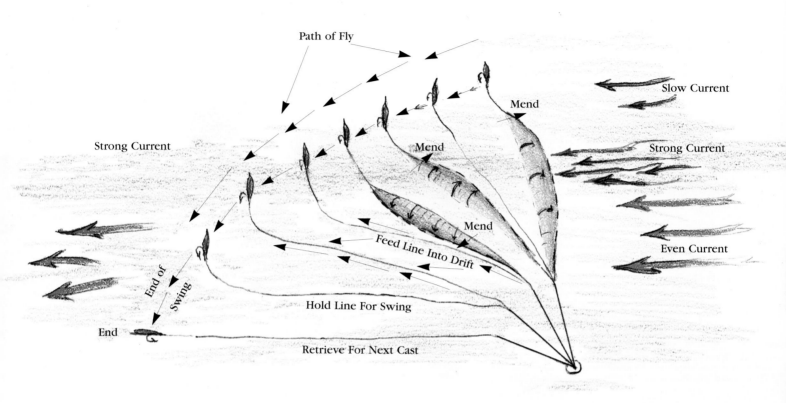

The Leading Swing or Greased-Line Swing
(Leading swing describes the energy of the presentation)
Leads fly down and across current
at the speed of the current, no tacking tension until the end.
Fly is seen full profile by the fish.

This presentation leads the fly across the current as if it were a baitfish swimming from one bank to the other while being carried downstream as it is swimming across. The fly always remains broadside to the flow and is seen in full length by the fish. It is similar to a cast and strip but the force of the current is used to move the fly, and line is fed into the cast through mending rather than being retrieved. The mending is a continuous process that lasts until the fly is hanging in the current directly below you. When the fly is moving faster downstream than the line, you mend the line downstream to slow it down and keep it broadside to the current. When the line is moving downstream faster than the fly, you mend it upstream so it will not pull the fly down. This is perhaps the most effective presentation to use when stripers are holding their positions and feeding on baitfish that are being swept into an area by tidal current.

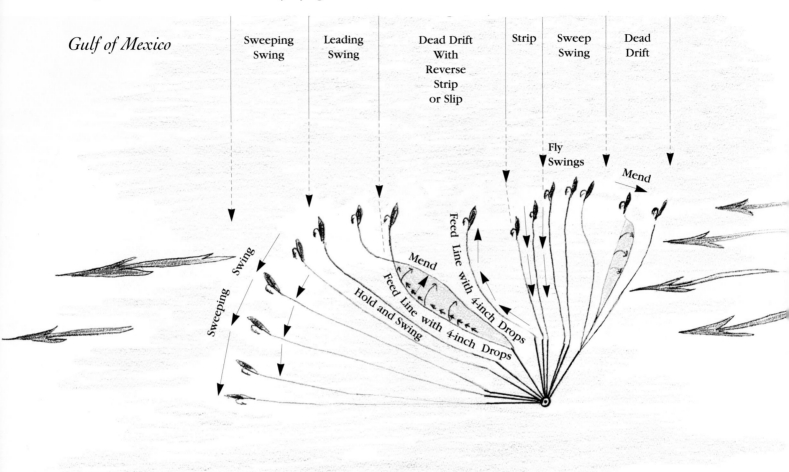

Slipping Drift

Using all methods in one cast to suit your fancy
or to fish the fly precisely "as you like it."
Use twitches and strips with leads and drops.
It is extremely effective.

This presentation incorporates all the previous presentations and uses the strip retrieve in reverse. The fly is cast across or slightly upstream and is mended to freely drift with the current. When it passes your position and begins to move downstream it is mended to swim broadside across the current with a leading swing and it is slipped down by feeding small amounts of line into the drift in such a way as to make the fly start and stop the opposite way that it would if you were stripping in line. When the cast is at its maximum distance below you, it is held and swung across the current with the classic wet-fly swing. Some form of this presentation is used in every cast you make. It will catch fish at every point because the line is always under control. As you gain experience in line handling you will find yourself using this presentation or some personal variation of it almost all the time. It is a great technique for albacore.

Deep-Drift Short Cast or Leisenring Lift

As effective as any technique for fishing deep with a fly rod can be.

1. Cast directly upstream.
2. Allow weighted fly to sink.
3. Hand line in slack fly line to keep in touch with still-sinking fly.
4. Raise rod to maintain control and feel.
5. As fly passes by, release line to keep the fly fishing deep holding the fly at depth.
6. Lower rod to continue.
7. Let fly rise to surface.
8. Flip fly upstream 2 feet further out and repeat until you have covered area to your satisfaction. Move upstream or downstream and repeat.

When this technique is executed with a short line with a long leader and split shot or a weighted fly it is as effective as any technique for fishing deep with a fly rod can be. The fly is cast upstream, allowed to sink as deep as it can, then the line is held and the fly will begin to swing towards the surface because of the force of the current. The upstream takes will usually be slight taps and they will come as the fly approaches the bottom. They are difficult to detect because the fish simply intercepts the fly as it moves toward him. After the fly passes by your position and the fly begins to rise up in the water, a fish is much easier to detect because the fish has to move to the fly rather than passively intercepting it. The long-leader technique can be used to fish deep with a great deal of control as to the depth your fly will fish and how it will move in the water. Sink tips are very effective with this technique especially with short leaders and weighted flies.

Pacific Ocean

Raise Rod and Keep in Contact with Fly

Short Cast, Weighted Fly

Checked Swing

Loose Leader Allows Fly to Sink Freely

Fast Current

CHAPTER 5

Single-Feather Flatwings:
An Intriguing Idea

Fly fishing is a discipline that is both an art and a craft. It has a long, well-documented history that has recorded and described many different fly-tying ideas and methods for using the materials available at the time to fashion and bring those ideas into visible form. Some of those ideas became popular and some did not. The worth of an idea was not always what made a fly attractive to tiers, it was rather the interest

the idea generated. Not many tiers have had the interest to see the worth of the flatwing streamer over the years and so its true value to the fly-fishing world has not been recognized or explored to a great extent.

Joseph D. Bates, Jr., in his book *Streamer Fly Fishing,* c 1950, mentions two flatwing streamers, the Cowee Special Streamer and the Nine Three streamer and states in passing that "very few flatwing streamers

haven't felt that feeling for a long, long time. I always wanted my flies to swim and look alive just like the baitfish did. Straight bucktail flies did a good job but streamers never satisfied my desire for imitation. They were stiff and opaque. The stems of the feathers did not allow them to swim naturally and although some of them were quite beautiful to look at, to me they never appeared alive in the water. I wanted a fly that would consistently catch fish without having to be pulled, yanked, stripped or tweaked in any way, shape or form. I wanted a fly that looked alive while at rest and also while it was moving. I wanted a miracle.

The answer, as it often is, was contained in the cause of the problem, the stem of the feather. I turned it sideways, tied it in flat as a tail just above the point of the hook and the fly swam in the water. I started to fish it and it did everything I had hoped for in a fly. It swam, it looked alive when at rest, it had the right silhouette, it lent itself to experimentation with color and materials and it caught fish consistently. I started to give them away with this admonition, "Hey, why don't you try one of these little flatwings, see how you like it." Those that tried them raved about the results, especially with difficult fish.

Flatwing streamers do one thing extraordinarily well and that is catch fish when other styles of streamers are in a slump. The profile of their wing causes them to glide through the water with a realistic suspending quality and they move with a side-to-side undulation that is remarkably lifelike.

The fly is tied by placing a small amount of bucktail on the aft portion of the hook to act as a platform to support the saddle hackle tail. Next a small amount of dubbing is placed around the thread that is holding the bucktail in place to act as a pillow to seat the stem of the first feather so it will stay in place and not twist when it is tied on. The first feather is tied in flat or horizontally and should be short and stiff and have the curved or dull side facing up. The energy contained within the upward curve of this feather will support and equalize the succeeding layers of feathers which are tied in flat with their curved sides facing down. The act of balancing the energy within the feathers causes the fly to become very sensitive to lateral pressure and the fly will shimmer and move from side to side with every touch of current. This method of constructing flatwings is at the core of creating a fly that will suspend and swim. The flat hackles act in a similar way to the wings of a paper airplane in that they both glide on a somewhat even plane. The hackles are not just for decoration but are an integral part of the swimming action of the fly.

The flatwing is a natural way of constructing flies to not only imitate the appearance of baitfish, but also their movement. They shine in difficult situations. When stripers are being selective and will not move

have been developed, but the idea behind them is so intriguing that it would appear that the reason for their lack of popularity is insufficient experimentation." He wrote that many years ago and he is still largely correct.

I don't know exactly when I started tying flatwings but I do remember the dissatisfaction I felt with the way streamers moved and looked in the water. I

from their feeding positions to chase flies that are being stripped past them, a well-placed flatwing will usually get a positive response. They work extremely well with traditional line-handling presentations that use the current as the force to deliver the fly to the fish. They swim and move as if they were alive without having to be pulled through the water. When a balanced flatwing is used with a dead-drift presentation it appears to be a living baitfish that is taking a rest as it is being carried downstream by the current. This quality of looking alive while at rest is one of the deadliest attributes of the flatwing. It enables the angler to fish for fish that are willing to feed but not willing to move. It also catches those fish that are willing to move but are particular about what they will move for.

You can alter the appearance of flatwings to imitate any minnow or forage fish you wish. They work well with a minimalist approach which is different than piling on materials. The water itself is the active ingredient that moves through the fly creating the inner pressures that cause the fly to swim. Be sure to leave room for it to flow. When tying in the layers of flat hackles remember that colors interact with each other and form secondary colors as the hackles move. When you use blue and place a yellow hackle on top of it you are making green, but you are still retaining both the blue and the yellow. This property of color can be very dynamic in the appearance of a fly under the water because it adds a quality of life and energy to the fly that appears natural. The body of a flatwing can be made with any material that suits your style of tying. One of my favorite flatwings, the Eel Punt, uses soft webby body feathers palmered down the shank of the hook for its body.

The body should reflect the appearance of whatever baitfish you are trying to imitate. The forewing or topping can be made with hackle or bucktail or any other material that suits your fancy. I prefer natural materials because I like the way they move and interact with each other. The collar is often tied in Deceiver style except that the forewing or top of the collar may be a hackle or some other material that imitates the back of a baitfish. I like to tie in an extremely sparse, long and flowing Deceiver-style collar of multicolored bucktail blended to interact and form secondary colors. I tie this to flare slightly and create the illusion of round

fullness. It works really well when imitating large baitfish such as mackerel, menhaden, herring or squid.

Flatwings are subtle flies, they are quiet, unobtrusive. Fish seldom take flatwings in a demonstrative way, rather they take them gently with seeming assurance. They move naturally in the water and lend themselves to traditional fly-fishing presentation techniques that are based on moving the fly to the fish through line handling.

Flatwings shine when used with dead drift and greased line presentations in moving water. They catch albacore extraordinarily well when they are slipped downcurrent with mending techniques. They catch fish with the hand twist retrieve in still water and they catch fish while they slowly sink along structural edges. They are not dramatic flies but they are very useful to the fisherman who likes too catch fish through his ability to understand and be in harmony with the fish's natural routines.

A good approach for tying flatwings for difficult fish is to match the size and general coloration of the baitfish. If you are fishing and are confronted with a situation where the fish are being selective and you do not have a fly that you feel comfortable with then remember that it is more important to have the fly act the same as the food the fish are feeding on than it is to have a perfect imitation. A good presentation in harmony with the feeding routine of the fish is a much better approach than a good fly with an incorrect presentation.

Correct presentation with a flatwing is simple, have the fly approach the fish the same way the food he is eating is approaching him and don't expect hammering strikes. The take, if you feel it, will be a light tap or a slight deadening in the feel of the line or a slight twitch in the leader.

Flatwing streamers are presentation flies. They work so well with selective fish that it is almost magical. They will catch fish with simple strip retrieves and they will catch fish with no imparted movement from the angler. Flatwings open up many possibilities to the observant salt water angler. Perhaps the intriguing idea of the flatwing streamer needed to find the vastness of the ocean to have the room it needed to grow and evolve towards the full scope of its true potential.

R.L.S. Nine Three

Flatwings

The flatwing streamer was first introduced many years ago. The most well known of the type is the Nine Three streamer and the Cowee River Special (Joe's Smelt). They are both tied with the feather (Cowee Special) or feathers (Nine Three) tied in flat at the head. They are very good flies and have caught countless fish since their introduction. The idea of tying streamer flies with the feathers tied flat is a very good one. They work so well on difficult fish that it is truly amazing. The flies that follow are simple flatwings. They differ from the original flatwing design in that the feathers are tied in at the tail rather than at the head. This simple change allows the fly to plane or suspend and swim with a lifelike side to side undulation.

Tying the One-Feather Flatwing

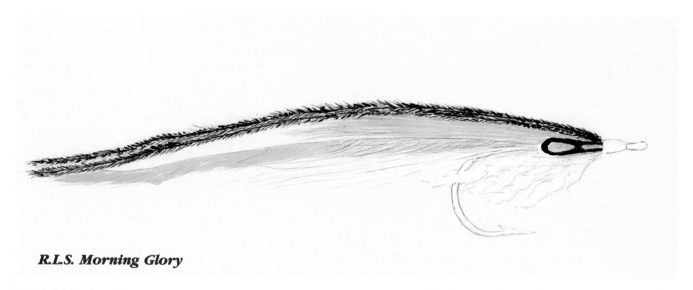

R.L.S. Morning Glory

R.L.S. Morning Glory
Length: As required.
Hook: 253NA, Eagle Claw, 1X short, all sizes.
Thread: White.
Tail: Small (30 hairs) bunch of white bucktail tied in long as a platform to support one, (1) long, thin and straight, yellow saddle hackle from a saddle patch (not strung).
Body: Gold Mylar braid.
Throat: Very sparse, fine white bucktail or small amount of white marabou, the length of the hook, tied to just veil the body and surround the bottom 2/3 of it. (you should be able to see the body easily through the fibers)
Wing: Apple green bucktail (30) hairs 1 1/2 times the length of the hook tied to surround the top third of the body.
Topping: 5 to 7 strands of peacock herl as long as the saddle.
Eyes: Jungle cock.

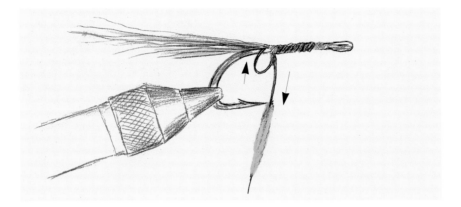

Hook: Place hook in the vice horizontally.

Thread: Start thread at the eye and fill in any gap between the shank and the eye, wind down to a point directly above the point of the hook.

Tail: Platform—The hairs of the bucktail are tied to support the saddle hackle and keep it suspended so it will swim with the slightest touch of current. This is done by spreading them to form a fan or broom shaped configuration. First, 30 of the longest hairs are separated from the bunch and are placed on top of the shank of the hook directly above the point. Cut the ends of the bucktail where you want the body to end to form an even underbody foundation for the gold Mylar braid to be wound upon. approximate distance from the point to the barb) Then wind the thread up to the cut ends and back down to just above the hook point. Next lift and spread the bucktail and slip the tying thread under it and pull it forward and tight to stiffen and support the hair in place as a platform.

◖

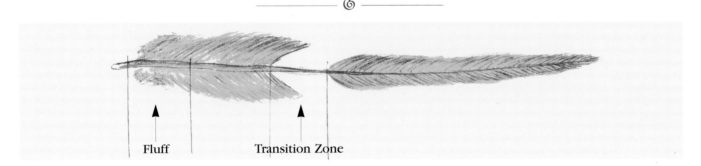

Fluff   **Transition Zone**

Next: *Tail:* Select a long, narrow, straight and thin stemmed saddle hackle from a yellow patch and hold it vertically by the butt of the feather. Ideally the feather will have a small amount of web running from the butt up its entire length. Notice where the shaft of the stem changes in thickness from the heavier butt section and tapers to the thin diameter that runs all the way to the tip of the feather. Strip the fibers off this transition zone leaving the stem bare for a half inch or more and do not cut the feather, leave it full length.

◖

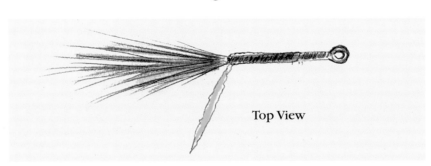

Top View

Tail: Take some of the fluff or marabou off the end of the feather and dub it onto the thread for about one inch.

Wind this dubbing around the shank of the hook exactly where the bucktail begins to spread (above the point of the hook). This forms a pillow or base to seat the saddle hackle in so that it will not twist when you tie it on.

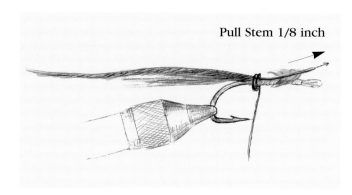

Pull Stem 1/8 inch

Tail: Slightly dampen and place the curved or dull side of the saddle hackle down flat upon the pillow with the bare stem parallel to the shank of the hook. Position the feather so that an eighth of an inch or so of the dampened fibers are covering the pillow. Then wind two gentle turns of thread around the feather to hold it in place.

Next: Look at the feather and adjust and correct its placement in such a manner to position it perfectly flat and straight and parallel to the hook shank. Then wind one or two turns of thread up the bare shaft of the feather and pull the stem of the feather slightly forward holding the tip of the saddle in one set of fingers and the stem in the other. This slight forward movement will seat the stem of the feather into the pillow and anchor it in place. It takes a little practice to do this but it is not difficult at all.

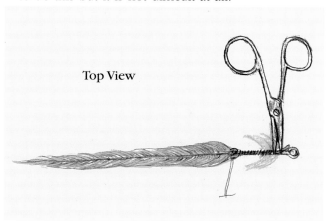

Top View

Wind the thread up the shank of the hook keeping the stem of the feather on the top of the hook and cut the stem at the end of the underbody, wind the thread back to the position just above the hook point.

Body: Tie in the gold braid on the bottom of the hook shank and wind the tying thread forward while keeping the tag end directly under the shank, cut the tag end of the braid and leave the thread positioned at the end of the underbody. Then wind the Mylar braid forward half lapping each previous turn and finish the body by tying the braid off on the bottom of the shank and then cutting off the end.

Throat: Very sparse, fine white bucktail, the length of the hook, tied to just veil the body and surround the bottom 2/3 of it (you should be able to see the body easily through the fibers).

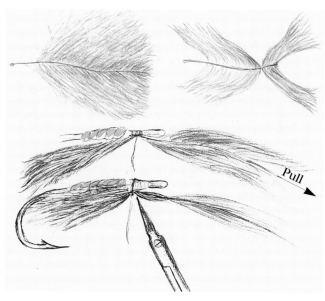

Alternate: Take a marabou plume with fine even fibers hold it upright and cut one inch or more of the stem in the center out with your scissors. This will leave a vee shape in the center of the feather. Turn the feather horizontal and hold it under the shank of the hook with the tips of the feather facing down the shank of the hook. (toward the bend) take a few gentle turns of thread positioning the fibers parallel to the body and pull the stem forward until the fibers are as long as the body, tie them off and cut the fibers behind the eye.

Wing: Bucktail, 15 hairs yellow, 15 hairs Apple green 1 1/2 times the length of the hook, mixed and tied to surround the top third of the body. Tie in the wing with two gentle turns of thread, then position the hairs and follow with the firm wraps as in the first section on tying hairwings. Cut the ends of the bucktail neatly into a taper.

Topping: 5 to 7 stands of untrimmed peacock herl either as long as the saddle or one third as long as the fly.

Eyes: Jungle cock.

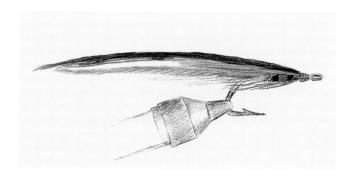

Neck Hackles

Spey Hackles

Saddle Hackles

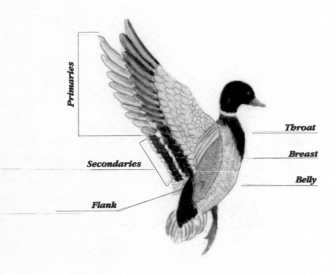

Primaries

Secondaries

Flank

Throat

Breast

Belly

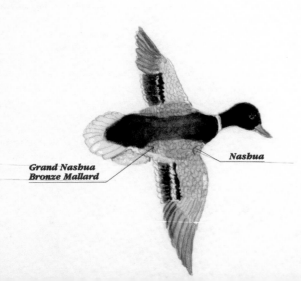

Grand Nasbua
Bronze Mallard

Nasbua

Feathers

The choice of a feather can
do much to enhance or
diminish the look of a fly.
Correct placement of
that feather with a
consciousness as to
its peculiarities may be
one measure of a fly tiers
true mastery of the
mechanics of fly tying.
No two feathers are
exactly alike although
there are major similarities
and ways of handling
these similar attributes.

Feathers are not created equal.
Feathers are feathers, true,
but some lend themselves
to fly tying and some do not.
Feathers can be and are; soft,
hard, glossy, webby, long, short, bent,
straight, lopsided, perfectly
symmetrical, asymmetrical, thin
stemmed, flat stemmed, twisted,
fat, skinny, or any combination
of these and more. Each
of these traits can be
dealt with effectively
to enhance a fly's
fish catching potential.
The way you tie each fly
will in some way be determined
by the feathers you choose
to build it with. The secret
is to take the time to look
at each feather and notice
its peculiarities and then decide
if it's uniqueness can be a help
or a difficulty which must
be dealt with and overcome
in order to fashion your creation.

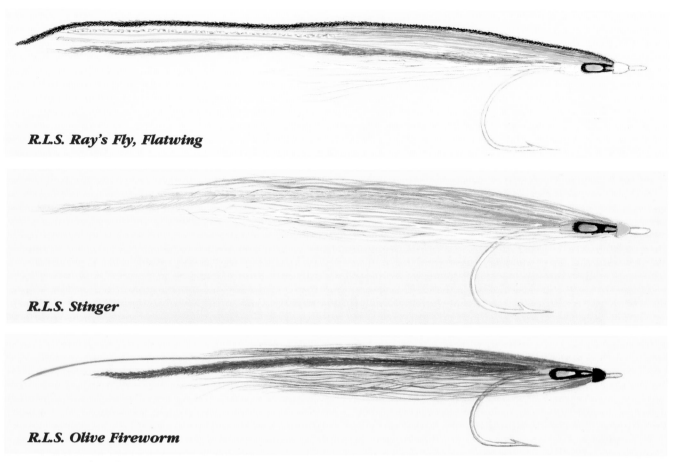

R.L.S. Ray's Fly, Flatwing

R.L.S. Stinger

R.L.S. Olive Fireworm

R.L.S. Ray's Fly, Flatwing

Length: As required.
Hook: 253NA, Eagle Claw, 1X short, all sizes.
Thread: White.
Platform: 30 hairs white bucktail.
Pillow: optional, white.
Tail: One long, medium wide olive saddle tied in flat, curve side down.
Body: Silver or pearl or gold Mylar braid.
Throat: Optional white marabou vee cut or white bucktail, sparse, the length of the hook.
Wing: Two strips of silver, or gold, or pearl Flashabou as long as the saddle under 30 hairs of white bucktail 1 1/2 times the length of the hook under 25 hairs of yellow bucktail 2 times the length of the hook under 2 strips of Rainbow Krystal Flash as long as the saddle under 25 hairs of olive bucktail 2 to 3 times the length of the hook.
Topping: Seven strands of peacock herl 1/2 to 1 inch longer than the wing.
Eyes: Jungle cock.

R.L.S. Stinger

Length: As required.
Hook: 253NA, Eagle Claw, 1X short, all sizes.
Thread: Yellow.
Platform: Bucktail, 30 hairs buff.
Tail: One long, narrow, light blue saddle, tied flat curve side down.
Body: Blue Mylar braid.
Collar: Bucktail, 30 hairs white, 2 1/2 times the length of the hook, tied to veil the bottom 2/3 of the body.
Wing: Bucktail, 30 hairs light violet 3 times the length of the hook.
Cheeks: Bucktail, 5 hairs of pink, fanned on each side, as long as the wing.
Eyes: Jungle cock.

R.L.S. Olive Fireworm

Length: As required.
Hook: 253NA, Eagle Claw, 1X short, all sizes.
Thread: Black.
Platform: Bucktail, 3 to 4 times the length of the hook, 10 hairs hot orange, 10 hairs yellow, 10 hairs chartreuse mixed.
Tail: One deep red, long and narrow saddle hackle, tied flat, curve side down under two strips of copper Flashabou one inch longer than fly.
Body: Chartreuse Mylar braid.
Collar: Bucktail, 20 hairs medium orange, 20 hairs deep red mixed, 2 1/2 times the length of the hook tied to surround and veil the bottom 2/3 of the body and flow into the tail.
Wing: Bucktail, 10 hairs of medium gray , 20 hairs of olive, 3 times the length of the hook.
Cheeks: Bucktail, 5 hairs chartreuse fanned on each side, as long as the wing.
Eyes: Jungle cock.

Catch and Release

Mixing colors can be done with feathers, saddle hackles in particular work very well. I like the effect produced by tying saddle hackles in flat, that is with the fibers on a horizontal plane especially in large flies. It gives them a lot of living color, so to speak, and the swimming movement of the feathers is spectacular. It does take a little practice to tie the feathers in correctly but how the flies swim and look is hard to beat for mimicking a live baitfish. When I imitate a large baitfish like a mackerel I never tie the fly exactly the same way twice. There are benefits to this approach but not everyone would agree.

I start by trying to visualize what the mackerel looks like while it is swimming through the water and also what it looks like when it suspends. I build the fly's body in silhouette rather than reproducing the appearance of mass through bulk. I'll tie in two or three white saddles, starting with a short neck hackle curve side facing up, then a longer saddle with the curve down. Then I add feathers to suit my present idea of how this particular mackerel should look. I may use a chartreuse feather, with a yellow feather on top of that and perhaps a silver doctor blue one over both of them, then a black or purple and perhaps a medium green one to top it all off. Maybe dyed grizzly maybe not. It is not a formula, it is a feeling.

I had one fly tied like this once that caught so many fish in one week that I gave it away for fear I would remember how I tied it and stop experimenting. Of course that fly wasn't tied exactly like this pattern. There are a few ingredients I left out and others I have forgotten but the idea is still there floating around in space. Catch and release fly tying. Maybe someday I'll run across it again and then again, maybe somebody else will.

For me this method of fly tying is satisfying because it allows access to creativity. It allows for freedom. It enables any tier to touch and feel the unknown intangible dimensions that do exist in nature but cannot be found by defined restrictions that bind access to accidental possibilities. These intangibles leave the domain of the unknown and become the known through the tiers imagination. They are not created through formula. Some flies fish better than others because of the skill of the person who made them and all flies always fish better in the hands of a skilled and creative angler.

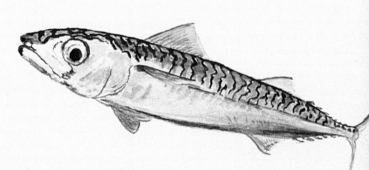

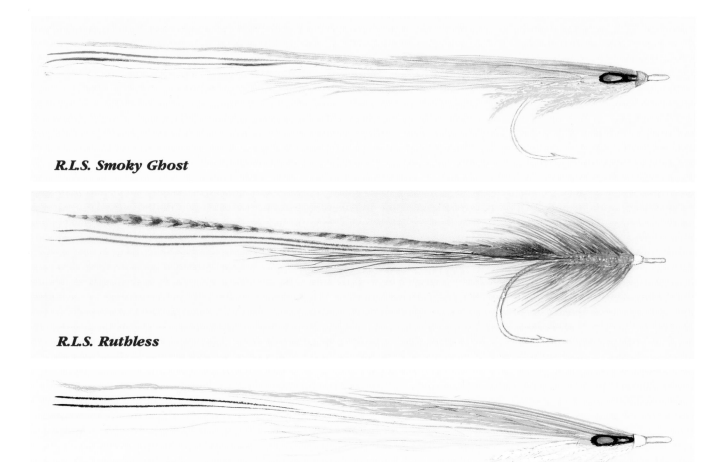

R.L.S. Smoky Ghost

R.L.S. Ruthless

R.L.S. Amber and Silver

R.L.S. Smoky Ghost
Length: As required.
Hook: 253NA, Eagle Claw,
  1X short, all sizes.
Thread: Gray.
Platform: Bucktail, 30 hairs pale
  gray.
Tail: 4 strands of Flashabou,
  2 strands of silver 1 of blue 1 of
  green under one long, narrow,
  thin stemmed bronze dun saddle,
  tied in flat, curve side down.
Body: Blue pearl Mylar braid.
Throat: Yellow marabou, as long
  as the hook, bottom and both
  sides (vee cut).
Wing: Bucktail, 10 hairs violet,
  10 hairs light gray, 5 hairs
  orange, 5 hairs fluorescent blue,
  2 times the length of the hook,
  mixed.
Eyes: Jungle cock.

R.L.S. Ruthless
Length: As required.
Hook: 253NA, Eagle Claw,
  1X short, all sizes.
Thread: White
Platform: Bucktail, 30 hairs of red.
Tail: Two strips of emerald green
  Flashabou under one long,
  medium wide, natural red
  grizzly saddle, tied flat, curve
  side down.
Body: Natural red grizzly,
  palmered five turns over gold
  Mylar braid.

R.L.S. Amber and Silver
Length: As required.
Hook: 253NA, Eagle Claw, 1X short,
  all sizes.
Thread: White.
Platform: Bucktail, 30 hairs pale gray.
Tail: 4 strips of Flashabou, 2 silver,
  2 purple under one long, narrow,
  thin stemmed yellow saddle hackle, tied flat, curve side down.
Body: Yellow pearl Mylar braid.
Throat: White marabou, as long as
  the hook, bottom and both sides
  (vee cut).
Wing: Bucktail, 10 hairs light gray,
  10 hairs honey, 10 hairs apple
  green 2 times the length of the
  hook, mixed.
Cheeks: Bucktail, 3 hairs of violet as
  long as the wing, tied as a clump.
Eyes: Jungle cock.

Theory of
Relativity

Consistency in tying flies does not come from formula but rather from being mindful of one's choice in materials. A pattern does not catch fish of itself. A pattern is a guide but the individual fly tier is the master tailor who uses the pattern as a starting point and makes the necessary alterations to make the fly fit the situation. Flies are ideas that can be altered to fit the need.

A fly pattern is never complete until it is in the water on a particular day. There are other factors that influence a fly's appearance and presence to fish besides its behavior, other forces that can never be defined or even touched through explanation come into play. The light, the grayness of the day, the slope of the bottom, the color and clarity of the water, all these and much more are meaningful to the fisherman who notices, all are somehow factors in his sensibility. They are like notes of music to a composer conductor. The music is the same yet each time the notes are played by the orchestra it is different. And it really is different.

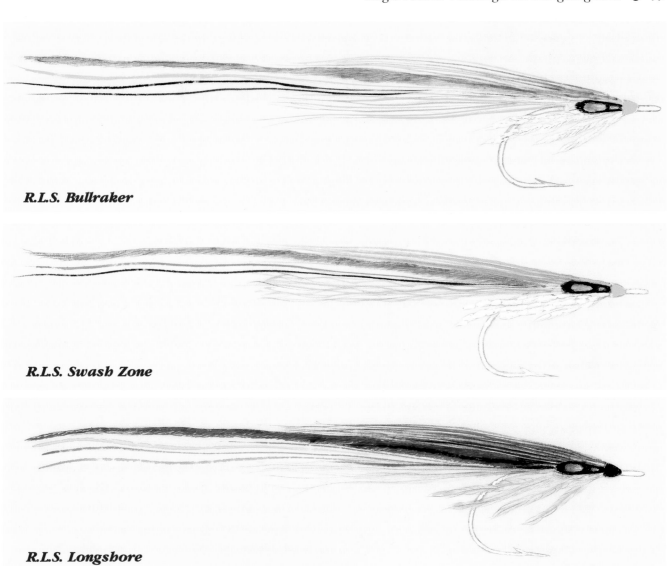

R.L.S. Bullraker

R.L.S. Swash Zone

R.L.S. Longshore

R.L.S. Bullraker
Length: As required.
Hook: 253NA,,. Eagle Claw,
1X short, all sizes.
Thread: Yellow.
Platform: Bucktail, 10 hairs white,
10 hairs fluorescent yellow,
10 hairs light blue.
Tail: 3 Strips Flashabou, 2 purple,
1 Chartreuse, under 1 long,
narrow olive saddle, tied flat,
curve side down.
Body: Silver Mylar braid.
Throat: White marabou, vee cut
as long as hook.
Wing: Bucktail, 15 hairs olive,
10 hairs tan, 5 hairs Chartreuse,
2 1/2 times the length of the
hook.
Eyes: Jungle cock.

R.L.S. Swash Zone
Length: As required.
Hook: 253NA, Eagle Claw,
1X short, all sizes.
Thread: Chartreuse.
Platform: Bucktail, 35 hairs pink.
Tail: 2 Strips of Flashabou,
1 violet, 1 blue, under 1 long
narrow blue dun saddle, tied
flat, curve side down.
Throat: White marabou, vee cut,
as long as hook.
Wing: Bucktail, 20 hairs light gray,
10 hairs light violet, 2 1/2 times
the length of the hook, mixed.
Cheeks: Bucktail, 3 hairs pink
each side, as long as the wing.
Eyes: Jungle cock.

R.L.S. Longshore
Length: As required.
Hook: 253NA, Eagle Claw, 1X short,
all sizes.
Thread: Black.
Platform: Bucktail, 15 hairs light
beige, 15 hairs light gray.
Tail: 3 Strips of Flashabou, 1 emerald
green, 1 turquoise blue, 1 gold,
under 1 long, narrow deep red
saddle tied flat, curve side down.
Body: Pearl Mylar braid.
Throat: Light beige marabou, vee cut,
as long as the hook. Wing:
Bucktail, 15 olive, 10 orange,
10 red, 2 1/2 times the length
of the hook, mixed.
Cheeks: Bucktail, 3 hairs emerald
green, each side.
Eyes: Jungle cock.

CHAPTER 6

Two-Feather Flatwings:
Henry T. and Hunky's Finest Kind

Flies are illusions, they may be inanimate objects when in a fly book but once they are in the water they have to be perceived by fish as living beings for them to be fooled. Spirit is what you are trying to imitate in a fly. If you sit long enough with the desire to understand this, it will come to you. You will understand something—intangible—on a wordless, bone deep level and that understanding can not be expressed through photographic realism. It can be approached, even touched but never quite captured because something essential is missing. It is the fisherman tier, who sees and knows with more than just his eyes who can appreciate this felt connection to the living being he is touching somehow along with his seeing. A fisherman who feels the spirit within the creature he is trying to imitate will tie flies that capture the essence of that creature and the fish he is trying to catch will see it too, because mysteriously it will be there.

Tiers who know this, know it in a way that is very often impossible for them to communicate in words, yet they can articulate it through their flies in a way that catches and holds the attention of fish. And this, of course, is the only true measure of their ability to perceive and act on the intangible as real and absolutely operational in fly fishing and fly design. This capacity is not as fully developed for some as for others but it exists in all fishermen and it always possible for any fisherman to engage it at any time. It is a feeling that leads to a state of awareness called savvy.

R.L.S. Henry T.

Two-Feather Flatwings

The first two feather flatwing we will tie is an excellent pattern for both the open ocean, tidal flows, surf and estuaries. It is simple to tie and incorporates Flashabou into the flat tail section of the fly.

R.L.S. Henry T.
Length: Tiny to large.
Hook: 253NA, Eagle Claw, all sizes.
Thread: White.
Platform: Small bunch of pale gray bucktail (30) hairs tied in long as a platform directly above the point of the hook, to support the flat hackles.

Tail: One (1) long, narrow, straight and thin stemmed, pale watery dun saddle hackle from a saddle patch. (not strung) Curved or dull side down. Two strips of silver Flashabou and two strips of chartreuse or light green Flashabou tied in directly above the point of the hook and on top of he stem of the dun hackle left long enough to extend beyond the tips of the dun feather by one inch. Next, one long, narrow, straight and thin stemmed grizzly hackle from a saddle patch tied in flat, curved side down, directly above the point of the hook on top of the four strips of Flashabou.

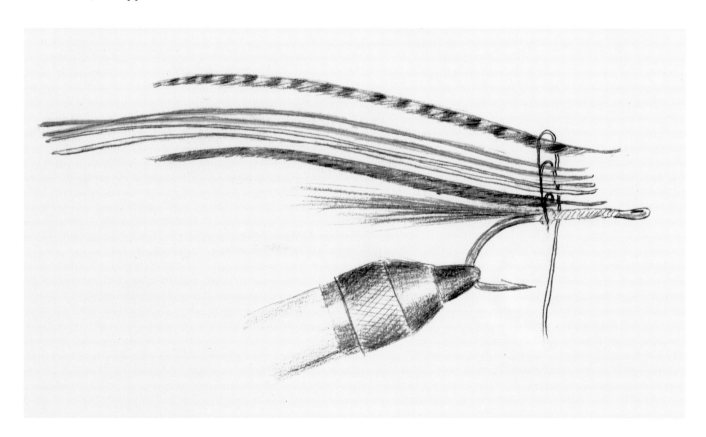

Note: Any time a feather will not lay flat, the use of dubbing as a pillow will usually solve the problem. Some feathers, however, are unmanageable because of idiosyncrasies in how they were formed. It is easier to change the feather than solve the engineering problem of how to get it to behave.

Body: Pearl Mylar braid.

Throat: Take a white marabou plume with fine even fibers hold it upright and cut one inch or more of the stem in the center out with your scissors. This will leave a vee shape in the center of the feather. Turn the feather horizontal and hold it under the shank of the hook with the tips of the feather facing down the shank of the hook. (toward the bend) take a few gentle turns of thread positioning the fibers parallel to the body and pull the stem forward until the fibers are as long as the body, covering the bottom 2/3 of it, tie them off and cut the fibers behind the eye.

This forms a white opaque gut that moves to allow the braid to shine as it is moved by the current.

Wing: Bucktail, 5 hairs of apple green bucktail, 5 hairs of medium olive, 5 hairs of dark olive, 3 hairs of fluorescent yellow, 3 hairs of fluorescent blue, 3 hairs of orange, blended together by your fingers from the tips, 1 1/2 times the length of the hook and tied to lay flat and surround the top third of the body.

Eyes: Jungle cock.

R.L.S. Hunky's Finest Kind

The second two-wing flatwing we will tie is a bit different. The body is tied with a technique called palmering which gives this fly the appearance of bulk without adding any physical mass. The fly is named in honor of Capt. Hunky Clark, the finest fisherman I have ever known.

R.L.S. Hunky's Finest Kind

Length: Tiny to large.

Hook: 253NA, Eagle Claw, all sizes.

Thread: gray or black.

Platform: 30 hairs of gray bucktail tied above the point of the hook.

Tail: One long, narrow, straight and thin stemmed grizzly saddle hackle from a patch. (not strung) Tied in flat, curve side down above the point of the hook. Two emerald green and two chartreuse strips of Flashabou tied in directly above the stem of the feather and above the point of the hook. Leave them long enough to extend beyond the tip of the grizzly feather by at least 1 to 1 1/2 inches if the fly is four to five inches long. Place another grizzly hackle directly on top of the Flashabou tie it in flat, curved side down.

Note: It is good practice to wind your thread over the cut ends of your materials with the idea of forming a neat underbody which will act as a foundation to shape the finish body. If you do this your flies will have symmetry and appear graceful. It is never a waste of effort or time.

The body on this fly is simple to tie. We will use a pale watery dun saddle hackle and palmer (or wind) it up the body in a series of five spirals, like a barber pole.

Body: Choose a pale gray saddle hackle with the fibers near the butt 1 1/4 to 1 1/2 times as long as the depth of the hook gap. Pick a feather that has webby or soft fibers that will lay back along the body and will move in the water easily. Strip the fibers off the butt and place and hold the feather on the bottom of the hook shank, the bare stem facing forward and the place where the fibers begin directly under the place where the tail is tied in. Have the curved side

Double
This
Section
on
Each
Turn

facing the fly and the feather in a lateral vertical position.

Fasten the stem of the feather securely and then place the pearl Mylar braid directly under it and secure. Wind the thread forward to the end of the underbody. Wind Mylar forward and tie it off on the bottom of the hook shank and cut off the excess.

Body: cont. Take the tip of the hackle between your fingers and thumb and raise t up to a vertical position, straight up from where it is tied in, and wet the tips of your fingers on your other hand. Gently draw the tips of your wetted fingers across the fibers pulling them back toward you while keeping tension on the feather by holding it taut by the tip. This procedure is called doubling a hackle. Wind the hackle forward in five evenly spaced turns, doubling it between each turn and winding each section of doubled hackle forward in five successive moves. Tie it off on the bottom of the hook. Trim the fibers and the stem cleanly and whip-finish.

Note: If you wish your flies to always look well formed there is a simple trick that will accomplish this. After finishing a fly, grasp the hook by the point, hold the head up and place it under hot tap water. The hot—not boiling—water will wet and soften the materials of the fly and they will take the shape that the flow of water gives them. Place them flat on a paper towel and let them dry undisturbed. They will retain the memory of how they dry; it gives them a permanent set.

Energy

To me, tying a fly is like painting a portrait.
I have such feeling to express. A fly is truly a
 combination of so many tangibles and intangibles. It
  is, the sky above it, the sun, the color of the light within
   the subject. It is the color of the light upon it and the
    fins and eye. It is those colors I don't see but know are
     there. And does the fish who sees it, care and do I? A fly
      that I tie is many things to me but never, ever is it just a
       pattern that I tie.

          A fly is a reflection of all the aspects I can know with-
           in the environment it is in. It is in the total environment. It is
            not a still life in a book. It is changing all the time and I try to
             reflect that change when I tie. That is why I mix and blend and use
              light and space and water as materials in my flies. So they will look and
               swim and my flies are only mine, nothing more, as yours are yours to do with
                as you will, my friend. It is of course "As You Like It," once again.

                 I like to tie so nothing is at rest within my flies. So that nothing is fixed, or rigid
                  or frozen. I like the red to wave within the fly and shift to violet then shift again. I like
                   the twitch I send down the line to bounce the fly and make it swim with purpose in
                    a fishes eye. Oh yes I do! And the touch of Krystal Flash catches the light so very lightly,
                     a glimmer that is all. And all one needs is just enough, no more no less, just right,
                      do not cross the line and over dress. No sizzle please just the meat, the real McKoy.
                       One strip of Crystal, No, make it two, and then deep in the middle of the wing
                        I want that silver there too, I think? Yes I do. And how do I know it will be seen?
                         I'll trust and leave some room for light to touch it and make it gleam. I need space
                          within the wing for water to flow through and make it swim as it should do,
                           and the sweep of colors that are there twinkle off and on, as they move
                            and touch each other in the wing or tail or veil or
                             in the cheek or throat or topping or anywhere at
                              all is fine, so very fine. But stiff and rigid
                               still life fly I do not tie, nor will
                                I buy or recommend.

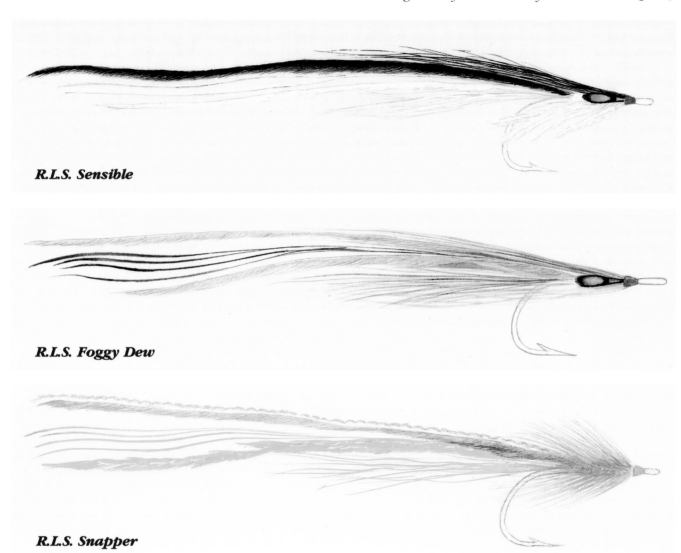

R.L.S. Sensible

R.L.S. Foggy Dew

R.L.S. Snapper

R.L.S. Sensible

Length: As required.
Hook: 253NA, Eagle Claw,
  1X short, all sizes.
Thread: Fluorescent red.
Platform: Bucktail, 30 hairs,
  fluorescent white.
Tail: 1 long, narrow white saddle
  under 2 strips of silver
  Flashabou under 1 long,
  narrow natural black saddle,
  tied flat, curve side down.
Body: Silver Mylar braid.
Throat: White marabou, vee cut,
  tied as a veil, as long as hook.
Wing: Black 30 hairs, 2 1/2 times
  as long as the hook.
Eyes: Jungle cock.
Note: All saddles are tied flat
  curve side down unless noted
  otherwise.

R.L.S. Foggy Dew

Length: As required.
Hook: 253NA, Eagle Claw, 1X short,
  all sizes.
Thread: Gray.
Platform: Bucktail: 30 hairs of gray.
Tail: 1 long, pale gray saddle under
  4 strips of Flashabou, 2 light violet,
  2 black, under 1 light blue saddle
  hackle.
Body: Rose pearl Mylar braid.
Collar: Bucktail, 20 hairs light violet,
  20 hairs light gray 2 times the length of
  the hook, mixed, tied to surround and
  veil the bottom 2/3 of the body.
Wing: Bucktail: 5 hairs of light violet,
  10 hairs of light blue, 10 hairs of medium
  gray, 5 hairs of light olive, mixed,
  2 1/2 times the length of the hook.
Cheeks: Bucktail, 3 hairs each side.
Eyes: Jungle cock.

R.L.S. Snapper

Length: As required.
Hook: 253NA, Eagle Claw,
  1X short, all sizes.
Thread: Yellow.
Platform: Bucktail, 30 hairs
  chartreuse.
Tail: Fluorescent yellow saddle
  under 4 strips of Flashabou,
  2 gold, 2 turquoise under
  turquoise saddle under
  4 strands of Chartreuse
  Krystal Flash.
Body: Palmered. Soft webby
  turquoise saddle palmered
  5 turns around a body
  formed of gold Mylar braid.

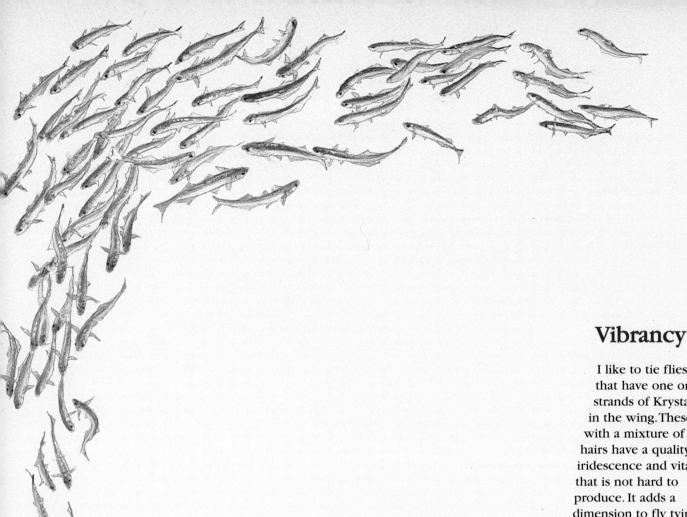

Vibrancy

I like to tie flies
that have one or two
strands of Krystal Flash
in the wing. These along
with a mixture of colored
hairs have a quality of
iridescence and vitality
that is not hard to
produce. It adds a
dimension to fly tying
that is very satisfying.
The colors one uses is a
matter of personal taste
and the sparser you tie
the more the colors will
interact and seem to glow.
The degree of sparseness
or translucency is subjective.
I like to be able to hold a
fly up to the light and see
through it easily. Flies that
block the light work, but
ordinarily I prefer not
to use them

There are times
when I want a bit more
of a color in a fly but I do not
want to change its overall "Look",
or visual feel. By using perhaps
only a single strand of that color in
Krystal Flash or Flashabou, I am able to
accomplish it easily or I may choose to add more
of a certain color hair that will mix with another color hair, say,
a light blue with some pink. This will produce a soft violet color while
retaining both the blue and the pink. Both of these colors have a good amount
of white in them they lighten up the overall look of the fly as if I had added white,
but with a difference . The white is not flat, it is an actively changing white because
of the mix between the pink and the blue tints and it adds a dynamic quality to
the appearance of the fly with little effort.

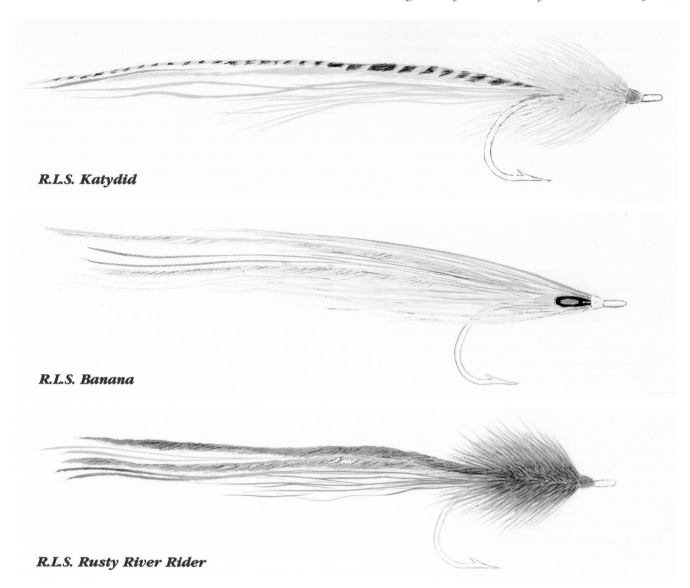

R.L.S. Katydid

R.L.S. Banana

R.L.S. Rusty River Rider

R.L.S. Katydid
Length: As required.
Hook: 253NA, Eagle Claw, 1X short, all sizes.
Thread: Chartreuse.
Platform: Bucktail, fluorescent yellow.
Tail: 2 strips of gold Flashabou under one yellow saddle under 2 strips of emerald green Flashabou under one yellow grizzly.
Body: Palmered. Soft, webby chartreuse saddle palmered over rose pearl Mylar braid.

R.L.S. Banana
Length: As required.
Hook: 253NA, Eagle Claw, 1X short, all sizes.
Thread: White.
Platform: Bucktail, light cream.
Tail: 2 strips of silver Flashabou under one off white saddle under 2 strips of green Flashabou under one long yellow saddle.
Body: Gold Mylar braid.
Collar: Bucktail, light cream, 2 times the length of the hook, tied to surround bottom 2/3 of the body.
Wing: Bucktail, 20 hairs of yellow, 20 hairs of orange, mixed 2 1/2 times the length of the hook.
Cheeks: Bucktail, 4 hairs of emerald green, 4 hairs of chartreuse.
Topping: Bucktail. 4 hairs of turquoise, 4 hairs of chartreuse, very long.
Eyes: Jungle cock.

R.L.S. Rusty River Rider
Length: As required.
Hook: 253NA, Eagle Claw, 1X short, all sizes.
Thread: Orange.
Platform: Bucktail 30 hairs orange.
Tail: 2 strips of copper Flashabou under one ginger saddle under 2 strips of gold Flashabou under dark or burnt orange saddle.
Body: Palmered. Soft webby, dark or burnt orange saddle palmered 5 turns over gold Mylar braid body.

Archetypes

Many fly tiers have been exposed to the blueprint schematic method of tying that has become popular through the efforts of popular tiers with a science background. This method of craftsmanship produces flies that are true wonders of mimicry, right down to the hairs on the top of the head, some are absolutely stunning and could and should be called works of fly tying art.

When this detailing is balanced with the dynamic appearance of life that can be achieved through loosening structure within a fly to allow movement to operate and complete the illusion, then there is more of a chance for a truly great fly to be fashioned.

The Muddler Minnow is a truly great fly in its simplest form. Add detail and it is not improved but it is not harmed either. The Gold Ribbed Hare's Ear stands on its own. It can be detailed but not harmed or improved. That perhaps is the measure of a great fly, that it retains its identity purely no matter what details are added to it. Its construction and grace represent life and the detailing adds a bit of something for someone in particular. The truly great flies are archetypes they can be altered and renamed by anyone but their identity can never be changed.

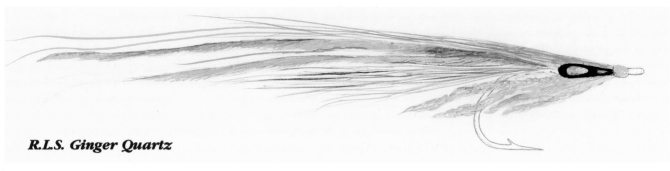

R.L.S. Ginger Quartz

R.L.S. Nuance

R.L.S. Avilar

R.L.S. Ginger Quartz

Length: As required.
Hook: 253NA, Eagle Claw, 1X short, all sizes.
Thread: Yellow
Platform: Bucktail, ginger.
Tail: One ginger saddle under 2 silver strips of Flashabou under one ginger saddle under 2 strips of gold Flashabou
Body: Silver Mylar braid.
Throat: Ginger marabou, vee cut, 1 1/2 times as long as the hook.
Wing: Bucktail, 25 hairs of ginger, 10 hairs of orange mixed, 2 1/2 times the length of the hook.
Cheeks: Bucktail, 2 light violet, 2 light blue, 2 light green, as long as the wing.
Eyes: Jungle cock.

R.L.S. Nuance

Length: As required.
Hook: 253NA, Eagle Claw, 1X short, all sizes.
Thread: Olive.
Platform: Bucktail, tan.
Tail: One tan saddle under 2 strips of green Flashabou under one olive saddle.
Body: Gold Mylar braid.
Throat: Tan Marabou, vee cut, 1 1/2 times the length of the hook.
Wing: Bucktail, olive.
Cheeks: Bucktail or substitute, 4 strands of fluorescent fuchsia (bright violet red).
Eyes: Jungle cock.

R.L.S. Avilar

Length: As required.
Hook: 253NA, Eagle Claw, 1X short, all sizes.
Thread: White.
Platform: Bucktail, white.
Tail: 2 strips of pearl Flashabou under one long narrow white saddle under 2 strips of gold Flashabou under one long narrow yellow saddle under 2 strips of black Flashabou.
Body: Pearl Mylar braid.
Throat: White marabou, vee cut, 1 1/2 times as long as the hook.
Wing: Bucktail, olive, 2 1/2 times as long as the hook.
Cheeks: Bucktail, 2 turquoise, 2 green, as long as the wing
Eyes: Jungle cock.

CHAPTER 7

Three-Feather Flatwings:
The Eel Punt

Some of my best flies are those that develop out of a theme that evolves over the course of several seasons of fishing. They are more of a mood about something than an imitation of something specific. The fly will begin in a feeling I have and then it will form into an idea that expresses my way of conceiving the energy of it. The first attempt may settle the whole thing and every fly I tie afterwards will be a variation of that first sketch.

I tie a fly I call the Eel Punt. It is a very effective fly and by that I mean it works all the time, throughout the season. It is a fly that is going to catch fish. It is a simple fly, three natural black saddle feathers tied flat, with a dark game bird hackle palmered body. This fly evolved over fifteen or more years.

My original idea was to tie a fly to imitate an eel and that wasn't difficult to do. It had to be black or dark and long and wiggle. There are many ways to do that and I tried every one I could think of and some of them caught fish really well. But I wasn't satisfied—confident yes, but not satisfied.

I began to tie using fur, strips of long silky fur. It was not rabbit fur, in fact I do not know what it was. It was soft, luxurious, with a sheen or luster that was simply rich. It came from a coat I was given by someone a long time ago. I cut the fur into strips, long ones and they worked very well. I tied bead-chain eyes in and painted them blue, it worked even better. Then I painted the hook blue and it even worked better. I still wasn't satisfied so I began to experiment with the shape of the strips and finally came up with a strip that was about one inch wide and seven or eight inches long and split the tail into three strips but left the first inch or so intact so it had three wiggly tails. Then I tied in a collar from the fur and bead-chain eyes. I used a double mono weed guard and it was complete.

It worked even better than I expected. It would glide down through the water slowly like a plane coming in for a landing. The whole thing looked just like anything you wanted to see. I caught everything on it from northern pike to bluefish, largemouths, stripers, fluke and more but I wasn't satisfied.

Then one day I knew what I wanted. I tied a little bit of blue bucktail on he hook for a platform and put three saddles down, palmered up a turkey body feather and put it in the water in some current and it swam. I showed it to some friends and they both said at the same time, "Hey! Look at that, it swims. Wow!"

So I was content, finally.

It's the best-catching eel fly I know of but you should use soft bird hackle for the palmering. Regular hackle works but not nearly as well. The natural black saddle hackle should be long narrow and thin stemmed and centered one on top of the other. This is a perfect presentation fly, a line handling finesse type of fly. You can strip it if you have the urge but it catches fish better while it just sits in the water sleeping or swimming lazily while sliding across the current at controlled depth with a greased line swing.

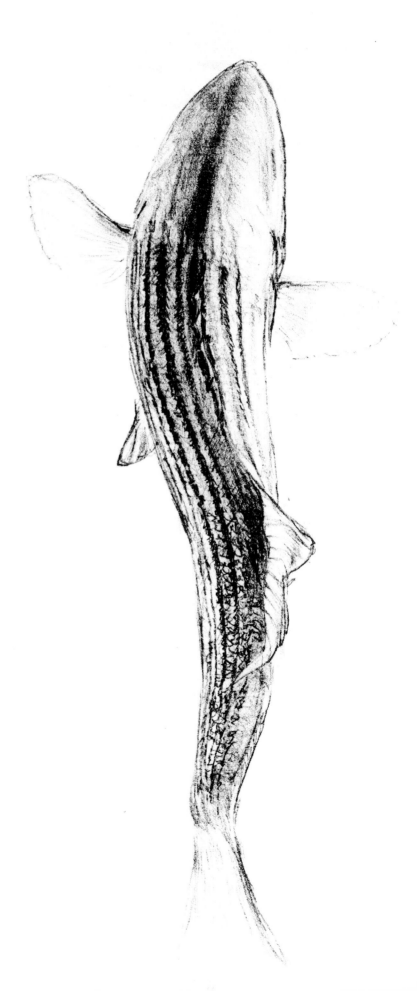

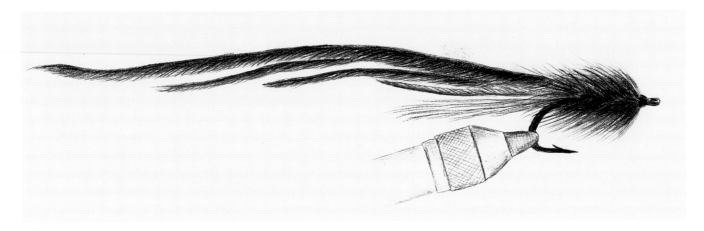

Three-Feather Flatwings

There have been more large stripers caught on eels than any other type of bait. Eels and striper fishing go together. They are the most consistent taker of large fish that has ever been used. There are times when other types of baitfish will produce better, still, when uncertain, an eel is never a foolish choice.

There have been many flies tied to imitate eels, all of them work and some of them work better than others. One of the best eel flies I have ever used is the Eel Punt. It is a simple fly that swims when properly tied. It works in the daytime and at night and is a good searching pattern when you are unsure of the feeding routines of bass.

Eel Punt

Length: As required.
Hook: 253NA, Eagle Claw, blackened or blued.
Thread: Black.
Platform: Bucktail, black or blue, tied to fan out horizontally like a broom.
Pillow: Black fluff from the base of a black feather

Support: One natural black neck hackle tied curve side up.
Tail: Three long, narrow, thin stemmed, natural black saddle hackles tied in succession, 1st. the shortest, 2nd. the middle, third, the longest. All tied flat, curve side down.
Body: Palmered. Any dark bird hackle that is long in the stem, or a long, soft, webby, natural black saddle hackle taken from the bottom back section of a saddle patch. Ideally, the feather that is palmered should have a webby fiber that holds its shape and resists the water yet is soft enough to move and look alive when used with traditional presentation techniques such as the Drag Free Float and the Greased Line Swing. Marabou is not a good substitute because it flattens against the hook when wet, it works b   ut does not add to the swimming motion of the fly.

Three feather flatwings have an extra mechanical step that balances the structural tension caused by the natural curve of the stem in the feathers used for the tail and helps the fly swim side to side freely.

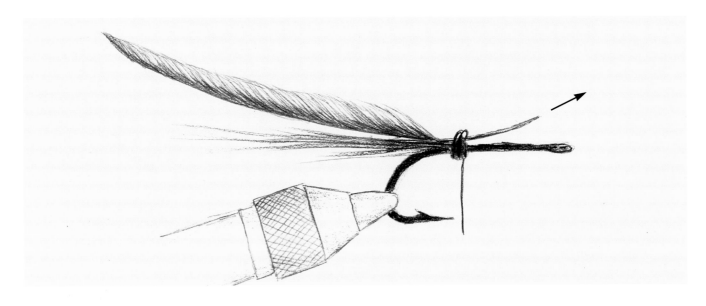

Tying steps for the Three-Feather Flatwing

Length: You are limited only by the length of the feathers you have available to you. Eels come in all sizes from two inch elvers to fully mature adults over four feet long. Flies from three to twelve inches long are the sizes commonly used with this style of tying because of the ease with which they can be cast.

Hook: 253NA, Eagle Claw, all sizes. This hook is made from carbon steel and is very light and strong. It is not expensive but adds a nice "look" to a fly. When it is used to tie the Eel punt it can be painted black which is not necessary but gives a visual harmony to the all black fly that a silver hook simply doesn't. It looks good.

Thread: Black. Wind the thread from the eye back to a point directly above the hook point.

Platform: Bucktail, The hairs of the bucktail should be placed and fastened just above the hook point. The butt ends should be left long so they can be trimmed at a point behind the eye (distance from barb to point) to form a smooth uniform underbody.

Pillow: Take a little tuft of the fluff from a black feather and dub it around the thread for about an inch. Then wind this dubbing around the base of the bucktail hairs just above the point of the hook. The pillow is a convenient way of dealing with the tendency of hackle stems to twist and not lay where you want them. The neck hackle that is used as the first feather in three wing flatwings has a stem that is ordinarily much thicker and often distorted in cross section. Using the little tuft of dubbing to seat the stem works very well. It works with the natural shape of the stem. Crushing the stem is a short lived solution that is undone quickly as the stem of the feather retains a memory and will relax back to its original configuration.

Support: This neck feather is a mechanical step that adds an upward energy to he tail that will, in conjunction with the bucktail platform, help to make the fly swim naturally. In larger flatwings the tail becomes more complicated through the addition of more layers of feathers and synthetics. It will hold its shape better and longer through the use of the support feather. Take a neck hackle from the center of any neck hackle of the right color and remove a single feather that is stiff and strong, approximately half as long as the full length of the saddles you choose for the tail. Remove the fibers from the first inch and dampen the butt end of the remaining fibers. Place the stem directly on the top of the pillow curve side up and wrap two turns of thread around it gently to hold it in place. The feather will lie along the top of the hook with an upward curve like a banana with its stem fastened. Grasp the tip of the feather with the tips of the fingers of one hand and the bare stem of the feather with the tips of the fingers of the other hand. Slowly pull the feather forward from the stem, holding the tip to insure that the feather does not move sideways, this will seat the stem in the soft dubbing exactly where you want it. Then wind a few turns of thread up the feather along the shank of the hook to secure it without moving the feather from its position by pushing it with the torque of winding the thread. Cut the stem of the feather at the end of the underbody and even it up by winding the thread forward and then back, returning it to the point just above the hook.

Tail: Take the shortest saddle and remove the first inch of fibers. Lay it on top of the neck hackle, curve side down and repeat the steps for securing the support feather. Repeat this for the second feather and the third. If you have a feather that has a difficult stem, form another pillow and simply seat the feather in the dubbing, if this doesn't work throw the feather away and choose another sometimes this is the best solution.

Body: Bird feathers are very soft and have a nice look when palmered. They are shorter than saddle hackles and you may have to use more than one to complete the body. Any dark feather seems to work very well with this fly. I have had great success with dark brown, dark gray and mottled feathers of various colors. Soft webby saddles work extremely well also it really is a matter of preference and convenience.

Start by tying in the feather at the bottom of the hook shank, stem directly under the shank and the curved side of the feather facing the hook. Wind the thread forward to the point that you believe the feather will reach when wound. Lift the feather by the tip and moisten the tips of the fingers of the other hand, hold the feather upright and draw the moistened fingers across he base of the feather pulling the fibers toward you. This does not have to be done perfectly, it is only a help called doubling a hackle and is a step hat many professional tiers never use. Wind the feather forward, either doubling between turns or continuously without that step. When you reach the place where the thread is located tie off the hackle on the bottom of the hook shank. If the fly needs more palmering simply repeat the steps tying in another feather on the bottom and working your way forward. Finish the fly by tying off the feather and forming a neat head. Whip finish with three sets of four turns each with waxed thread or several half hitches and head cement.

Perception

Fly tying is an art.
If it could be called a science
it is one that is subject
to our feelings, desires,
our imagination and
our personal loves
and hopes.
It reflects our grace
in discerning form
and order in nature
and our ability to create
an illusion that may reflect
what we have perceived
to be the "Look",
of what we wish
to mimic.
The art in fly tying
is unique in that
it engages
the predatorial side
of nature as its audience.
It seeks to touch
the awareness
of non-human beings,
move that awareness
into fixed attention,
and then use
this non-human trance
to accomplish
a predatorial human goal,
the catching of a fish
through the use
of illusion.
This in and of itself
is a most interesting insight
into our true role
as a force
within the balance
of natures balance.

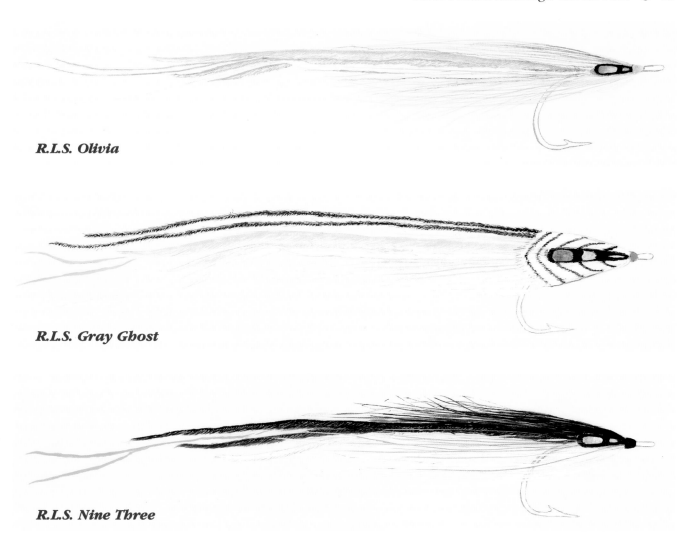

R.L.S. Olivia

R.L.S. Gray Ghost

R.L.S. Nine Three

R.L.S. Olivia

Length: As required.
Hook: 253 NA, Eagle Claw.
Thread: Chartreuse.
Platform: Bucktail, ginger.
Pillow: Dubbing, ginger.
Support: White neck hackle.
Tail: first, ginger, second, 2 strips of pearl Flashabou, third, ginger, fourth, 2 strips of violet Flashabou, fifth, light blue.
Body: Violet Mylar braid.
Collar: Bucktail, ginger.
Wing: Bucktail, a mix of light, medium and dark olive.
Cheeks: Bucktail, 5 hairs of violet, 3 hairs of pink.
Eyes: Jungle cock.

R.L.S. Gray Ghost

Length: As required
Hook: 253 NA, Eagle Claw.
Thread: White.
Platform: Bucktail, white.
Pillow: Dubbing , white.
Support: White neck hackle.
Tail: first, white, second, 2 strips of silver Flashabou, third, pale gray, fourth, 2 gold strips of Flashabou, fifth, light blue gray saddle.
Body: Orange Mylar braid.
Collar: Bucktail, white.
Wing: Bucktail, light blue gray.
Cheeks: 3 hairs turquoise, 3 hairs pink both sides covered by silver pheasant white and black barred feathers, one on each side.
Topping: 7 strands of peacock herl.
Eyes: Jungle cock.

R.L.S. Nine Three

Length: As Required
Hook: 253 NA, Eagle Claw.
Thread: Black or white.
Platform: Bucktail.
Pillow: Dubbing, white.
Support: Neck hackle, white.
Tail: First, white saddle, second, light olive or bright green saddle, 2 strips of gold Flashabou, third, black saddle.
Body: Silver or pearl Mylar braid.
Collar: Bucktail, white.
Wing: Bucktail, black, dark blue, purple, mixed 2 1/2 times the length of the hook.
Cheeks: Bucktail, 9 hairs, 3 pink, 3 yellow, 3 light blue.
Eyes: Jungle cock.

Seeing

Seeing things well is a process that reveals and unfolds hidden truth as
our insight and understanding increases. There is always more to see and learn
unless we refuse to remain open to nature's secrets.
Fly tying is one way we can experiment with our ability
to observe and mimic what we have seen.
The fish will tell us how well we have seen or
if we have been seduced once again by our own,
or someone else's, illusions.

There are many ways to look at things and
at the moment of seeing them we may conclude
that what we see is the fact, the truth
of what they look like. Our conclusion can be
nothing more than a projection
or illusion based on our opinion as to
the fullness of what we have witnessed or
the limitations on our view that we
are not aware of.
What we see is what we notice,
a particular view from a
particular perspective.
It is never false but
it is not the full
picture of what
we are looking at.
Beauty resides
everywhere.
The desire
to see it is
never less
than enough.

R.L.S. Skinny Mack

R.L.S. Supervisor

R.L.S. Sure Thing

R.L.S. Skinny Mack

Length: As required.
Hook: 253 NA, Eagle Claw.
Thread: Yellow.
Platform: Bucktail, white.
Pillow: Dubbing, violet.
Support: Violet neck hackle.
Tail: First, yellow grizzly, second,
    2 strips of light blue Flashabou,
    third, violet grizzly, fourth,
    2 strips of gold Flashabou, fifth,
    light chartreuse grizzly or light
    green grizzly.
Body: Violet Mylar braid.
Collar: Bucktail, white on bottom,
    yellow on the sides.
Wing: Bucktail, 10 hairs each,
    turquoise, emerald green, yellow,
    black, 2 1/2 times as long as the
    hook.
Cheeks: Bucktail, 5 hairs pink, each
    side.
Topping: 7 strands of peacock herl.
Eyes: Jungle cock.

R.L.S. Supervisor

Length: As required.
Hook: 253NA, Eagle Claw.
Thread: White.
Platform: Bucktail, white or red.
Pillow: Dubbing, white or red.
Support: Neck hackle, white or
    red.
Tail: First, white, second, very
    light pale blue, third, short,
    light green, 1/2 as long as the
    second feather.
Body: Pearl Mylar braid.
Collar: Bucktail, white.
Cheeks: Bucktail, 3 hairs pink,
    3 hairs fluorescent yellow.
Topping: 5 hairs of light blue
    and light green bucktail
    mixed under 7 strands of
    peacock herl.
Eyes: Jungle cock.

R.L.S. Sure Thing

Length: As required.
Hook: 253NA, Eagle Claw.
Thread: Yellow or white.
Platform: Bucktail, white.
Pillow: Dubbing, white.
Support: White neck hackle.
Tail: First, 2 strips of gold
    Flashabou, second, white
    saddle, third, 2 strips of red
    Flashabou, fourth, either a
    ginger or a yellow saddle, fifth,
    2 strips of emerald green
    Flashabou, sixth, a yellow saddle
    (Flashabou extends 1 inch).
Body: Gold Mylar braid.
Collar: Bucktail, bottom white,
    sides, light beige or light
    yellowish tan (ginger).
Wing: Bucktail, yellow, 2 1/2
    times the length of the hook.
Cheeks: Bucktail, 3 hairs emerald
    green, 2 hairs turquoise.
Eyes: Jungle cock.

Incomprehensible Reasonability

There are ways to explain and define many types of phenomena.
All of them are true within their limited view and when these boundaries are breached
there is always more to learn and see. When more information is known,
the definitions of what is true expand.
Definitions do not lend themselves to openness and wonder at the mysteries of Nature,
rather, they put closure on them. We do have an innate drive to quantify everything,
to label and categorize endlessly based on the information we have access to.
"Bees can't fly," is a perfectly reasonable statement based on the laws of flight
that once were understood as operational, and yet bees flew anyway
in spite of the reasonable explanation that they couldn't.
There is nothing wrong with trying to understand
but there is something wrong with disregarding what our senses tell us is occurring.
Explanations may give our minds comfort but they are always less than what is really going on.
Accepting explanations as limited viewpoints without closure frees a person to wonder and imagine,
to enjoy and experience what they care about rather than be bound
by having to know why everything is exactly the way it is.

Ideas are explanations not the experience itself. There is always more to learn and in the process,
ideas change but the experience always contains every explanation possible.
The currently fashionable scientific explanation that the color violet penetrates most deeply
into the depths of the ocean and the color red has the least penetration
desregards the fact known to all artists that violet without red remains true blue.
The experience of seeing violet includes seeing red no matter what the depth.
"I would rather live in a world surrounded by mystery than in a world limited to the inventory of my mind."

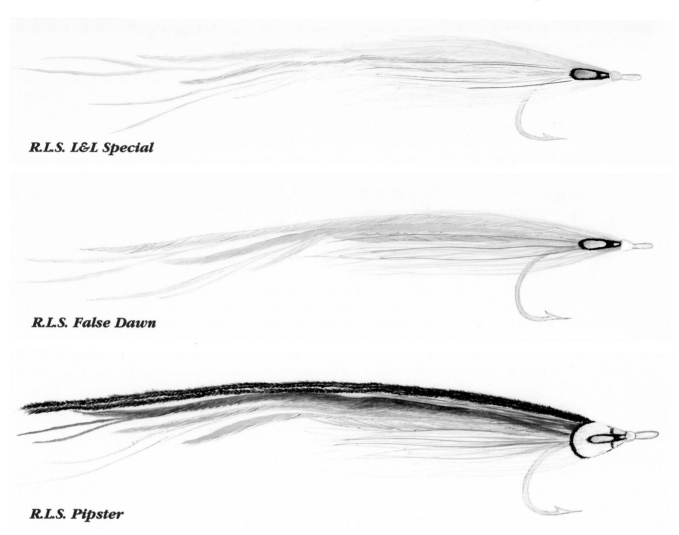

R.L.S. L&L Special

R.L.S. False Dawn

R.L.S. Pipster

R.L.S. L&L Special
Length: As required.
Hook: 253 NA, Eagle Claw.
Thread: Chartreuse.
Platform: Bucktail, fluorescent
   yellow.
Pillow: Dubbing, yellow.
Support: Chartreuse neck hackle.
Tail: First, white saddle, second,
   2 strips of silver Flashabou,
   third, chartreuse saddle, fourth,
   2 strips of gold Flashabou,
   fifth, fluorescent yellow saddle.
Body: Silver or pearl Mylar braid.
Collar: Bucktail, bottom,
   fluorescent white, sides
   fluorescent yellow.
Wing: Bucktail, chartreuse.
Cheeks: Bucktail, 3 hairs
   turquoise, 3 hairs violet.
Eyes: Jungle cock.

R.L.S. False Dawn
Length: As required.
Hook: 253 NA, Eagle Claw.
Thread: White.
Platform: Bucktail, light blue.
Pillow: Dubbing, light blue.
Support: Light blue neck hackle.
Tail: First, pale light blue saddle,
   second, 2 strips of light blue
   pearl Flashabou, third, light blue
   saddle, fourth, 2 strips of gold
   Flashabou, fifth, pale light blue
   saddle.
Body: Gold Mylar braid.
Collar: Bucktail, light blue.
Wing: Bucktail: light blue
Cheeks: Bucktail, 3 hairs
   turquoise, 3 hairs yellow.
Eyes: Jungle cock.

R.L.S. Pipster
Length: As required.
Hook: 253 NA, Eagle Claw.
Thread: White.
Platform: Bucktail.
Pillow: Dubbing, white.
Support: Yellow neck hackle.
Tail: First, yellow saddle, second,
   2 strips of pearl Flashabou, third,
   chartreuse saddle, fourth, 2 strips
   of red Flashabou, fifth, olive saddle.
Body: Red Mylar braid.
Collar: Bucktail, bottom white, sides
   light blue.
Wing: Bucktail, light olive.
Cheeks: Bucktail, 3 hairs pink, 3 hairs
   turquoise, 3 hairs yellow covered by
   Lady Amherst pheasant tippet
   feather, pulled forward by the
   stem to form an eye spot, one
   on each side.
Topping: 7 strands of peacock herl.
Eyes: Jungle cock.

CHAPTER 8

Squid

Squid are creatures of myth. We have a fascination with them. Sagas of the sea have the obligatory encounter with a giant squid whose rubbery suction-cup-laden arms envelop the damsel in distress and pull her towards a snapping beak while a malevolent eye watches the handsome hero chop off its tentacles fifty at a time. Jules Vern, author of *Twenty Thousand Leagues Under the Sea,* appropriately names his underwater boat after a cuttlefish with a ballast tank, the Chambered Nautilus. The squid who live in our cultural imagination are strange almost other-worldly beings with alien predatory powers. Thank God we have stripers to keep their numbers in check.

Long fin squid and Boreal squid are the common species found along the East Coast. They are predatory and feed on the same species of baitfish that game fish eat. They travel in schools or formations and move as a unit through the water. When they are feeding they move under the bait, pick out their victim and dart up from underneath and grasp it with their tentacles. They move forward in the water with their eyes and arms located in the front. They propel themselves by undulating their fins and can quickly reverse their direction by reversing the undulation. They are extremely fast and can move with such speed that the eye cannot follow their movement. Most of the time they move slowly and evenly, at times almost imperceptibly as they hunt for prey. To the untrained eye they do not look like squid at all. They appear to be a school of fish hovering in the water.

Newcomers to striper fishing may not be aware of the effect the presence of squid has on stripers. This is understandable because squid give few clues as to their presence when they are around. They are discrete and they are wary. Some fishermen believe they are intelligent, I am one of those that do.

Stripers like to eat squid. When squid appear bass will alter their feeding pattern and begin to take squid when they get an opportunity. You may not notice the squid right away but the bass do and their behavior will change somewhat. Once in a while you will see a fish come out of the water. This jumping is a clue but it is easy to overlook when bass are feeding on the surface. Most of the time bass do not jump out of the water even when feeding, there will be swirls and breaks but seldom do you see the fish itself. Another clue that can alert you to the presence of squid is the force in the rise form of the breaking fish. Stripers put it in high gear when they go after a squid. They don't ordinarily chase them over a distance, they pick one out, move under it, zero in, then when they are in split second range, let go with every inch of speed they have and try to catch the squid before it can move. This speed transmits itself in their rise. The water churns, sometimes the fish comes right out, and often a loud pop accompanies a tight, swirling boil. I think the squid get away most of the time.

You would think that this type of aggressive feeding would translate into arm-wrenching strikes but surprisingly it doesn't. A light tap is all you will feel. You cast out your fly, retrieve it slowly with the old-fashioned hand twist, wait for the tap, tighten, and hopefully set the hook. If you set too quickly you will come up empty every time. That first tap is the fish flaring its gills and inhaling the water in which the squid is swimming. You have to wait for the fish to close its mouth and every fish is a little bit different in their timing. Fast retrieves are easier to hook fish with but sometimes the fish will not co-operate. It is best to learn how to catch the bass using both methods rather than limiting yourself to the easier fast retrieve.

Squid can alert you to their presence with a few subtle signs. The most common clue is they will hit your fly. They seldom get hooked but the feel of the hit is unmistakable once you learn to recognize it. It is not strong. It is a little bit of back pressure sometimes, other times it is like series of fumbling taps or tweeks or twitches. They grab the fly, then let it go, then grab it again, and so on, they just touch it. If your fly was on the bottom you would think that a crab was after it.

Another clue to their presence is the way they feed. They swim up under their prey and grasp it in their arms. When the prey is swimming at the surface and squid are feeding on them there, you will see little twitching splashes where their tentacles break the surface as they wrap around the baitfish. It looks like someone was throwing pebbles into the water with a little skip, it is very quick and minimal.

The last way to know if squid are present is to see them. They ghost along under the surface and if there is any light their heads will reflect it with a whitish glow. If you are fishing the surf, they will be located just on the outside of the first line of breaking waves or along the first noticeable depth change or breakline. They will be swimming parallel to the shoreline and will appear as faint shadows or reflections.

When tying squid flies it is hard to resist emphasizing their tentacles or their eyes because it is how we have been taught to view them since childhood. When we see them as they actually appear in the water they are quite different than what cultural conditioning says they are.

Fishing blind with a squid fly will bring results. Stripers seem to relish them so it is always worth your while to give them a try. There are many patterns designed to imitate squid and you may have success using them. My personal preference is the Razzle Dazzle, the Banana Squid or any lightly dressed flatwing streamer five to ten inches long with a wide, long saddle hackle tail and a flared collar of bucktail tied Razzle Dazzle style with muted colors. Be creative.

Squid flies are a good choice to make when you have the desire to try and catch a very large striped bass. Huge stripers often take a properly presented squid fly when they will not move or respond to anything else. The largest striper I have ever caught on a fly rod came to an orange squid fly on a bright spring afternoon in an estuary. I have learned to have faith in the possibilities that squid flies present to an angler. Squid flies work. Try them, the rewards are great and don't forget to set the hook before you get the line on the reel, it's the best time to do it and it may be the only chance you are going to get.

Squid

Squid have the ability to change their color to blend
with their surroundings. They can instantaneously turn
into a checkerboard pattern if they have the need. They can
blink colors on and off like a strobe light, going from blue to
amber to violet to red to clear and they can do it in less time
than it takes to register in your mind. Squid come in every
color and they change these colors at will, both to camouflage
themselves and to communicate with each other. Their
natural color is a translucent amber and it is the color
they display when they are at ease.

Their shape is always the same. It is an elongated
cigar or banana shape, pointed at both ends
with the eyes and tentacles at the front.
Squid use their tentacles which are held
tightly together as a forward facing steering
rudder. They propel themselves by
undulating their fins and steer from
the front where their eyes are located.

Their translucency makes them hard
to see in the water. They appear as a
vague shape with a slight glow,
very indefinite in appearance.
Their vagueness is their trademark
and flies tied to imitate them
should reflect this appearance
when in the water.

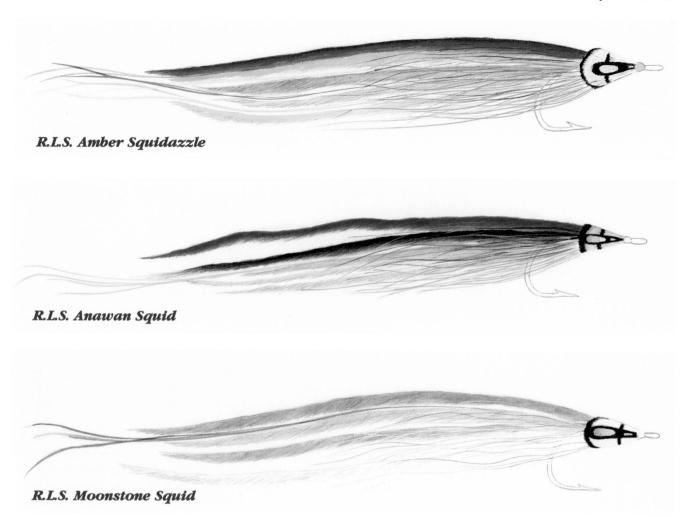

R.L.S. Amber Squidazzle

R.L.S. Anawan Squid

R.L.S. Moonstone Squid

R.L.S. Amber Squidazzle
Length: As desired.
Hook: 253 NA, Eagle Claw.
Thread: Yellow.
Platform: Honey bucktail.
Pillow: Dubbing, light gray.
Support: Light gray neck hackle.
Tail: First, pale yellow saddle, second, 2 gold Flashabou, third, a gray saddle, fourth, 2 red Flashabou, fifth, a ginger saddle, sixth, 2 pearl Flashabou, seventh, a pink saddle, eighth, 2 light blue Flashabou.
Body: Light violet Mylar braid.
Collar: Bucktail, honey on bottom, honey, orange, blue and chartreuse mixed together on the sides.
Wing: A wide, medium brown saddle or neck hackle.
Cheeks: Lady Amherst pheasant tippet feathers one on either side.
Eyes: Jungle cock; placed to center against the tippet feather.

R.L.S. Anawan Squid
Hook: 253NA, Eagle Claw.
Thread: White.
Platform: Yellow.
Pillow: Yellow.
Support: Yellow neck hackle.
Tail: First, a pale gray saddle, second, a chartreuse saddle, third, a wide ginger saddle, 4 strands of gold Flashabou, fifth, a furnace saddle.
Body: Gold Mylar braid.
Collar: Bucktail, ginger on bottom, ginger, yellow, orange and turquoise on sides.
Wing: Deep red saddle.
Cheeks: Golden pheasant tippet, one on each side.
Eyes: Jungle cock, centered.

R.L.S. Moonstone Squid
Hook: 253NA, Eagle Claw.
Thread: White.
Platform: Fluorescent white
Pillow: Dubbing, yellow.
Support: Yellow neck hackle.
Tail: First, a fluorescent white saddle, second, a light pink saddle, third, 4 stands of Flashabou, one each of copper, red, gold and emerald green, fourth, a wide pale gray neck or saddle hackle.
Body: Pearl Mylar braid.
Collar: Bucktail, fluorescent white on bottom, fluorescent white, purple, turquoise and fluorescent yellow on sides.
Wing: A violet saddle
Cheeks: Lady Amherst pheasant tippet, one on each side.
Eyes: Jungle cock, centered.

Intuition

I like intuition. It teaches me. It makes me become aware of things I know but do not know I know.
It comes somehow and arrives full grown and I feel it in my whole being and yet I cannot define it. It's a
feeling, a sort of, kind of knowing feeling, one that you can't quite understand but if you don't act on, you
always regret. The kind of regret that comes when you don't buy flowers for someone when you want to.
It's a loss, an irreplaceable one, and yet, it never exists except in a feeling, a feeling of missing something that cannot ever be experienced because the time for it is gone.

Intuition is a word that refers to a state of knowing something in such an
unfamiliar way that many of us choose to ignore its value and
fail to recognize its silent power. It is a state
of being that one can learn to
cultivate and be aware of.

Intuition is not speculation
or thinking nor is it meditating
or contemplating. It definitely
comes upon you unawares.
It's an all-of-a-sudden kind
of thing, like a cool breeze
you weren't expecting on
a hot and sultry day or a
deer that walks right up
to you and gives you
a sniff. It's a gift.
To recognize and know that
it is a gift is to begin
to get in touch with the
mystery that we are and
live within. We can try to
understand it but that only
serves to bind it to words
and words cannot contain
it and so it slips away and
hides from that approach.
Understanding with the
mind is not the path to
intuition. Give yourself
the freedom to feel
and you will be
rewarded beyond
your wildest
dreams.

R.L.S. Blue Moon Squid

R.L.S. Cold Fury

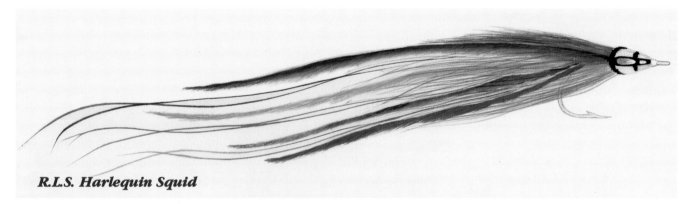

R.L.S. Harlequin Squid

R.L.S. Blue Moon Squid

Hook: 253NA, Eagle Claw.
Thread: White.
Platform: Buff.
Pillow: Dubbing, off white.
Support: Off white neck hackle.
Tail: First, an off white saddle (pale tannish white), second, 2 gold Flashabou, third, a wide off white saddle, fourth, 4 strands of Flashabou one each red, emerald green, blue and silver, fifth, a wide pale blue saddle.
Body: Pearl Mylar braid.
Collar: Bucktail, buff and pink, bottom and both sides.
Wing: Bucktail, light blue.
Cheeks: Lady Amherst tippets.
Eyes: Jungle cock

R.L.S. Cold Fury

Hook: 253 NA, Eagle Claw.
Thread: Hot orange.
Platform: Hot orange.
Pillow: Hot orange.
Support: Hot orange neck hackle.
Tail: First, a hot orange saddle, second, 2 strands of emerald green Flashabou, third, a fluorescent yellow saddle, fourth, 2 strands of light blue Flashabou, fifth, a hot orange saddle.
Body: Silver Mylar braid.
Collar: Bucktail, mixed hot orange and fluorescent yellow, bottom and both sides.
Wing: Bucktail, fluorescent yellow.
Cheeks: Golden pheasant tippets.
Topping: Turquoise saddle.
Eyes: Jungle cock.

R.L.S. Harlequin Squid

Hook: 253NA, Eagle Claw.
Thread: White.
Platform: White.
Pillow: Dubbing, yellow.
Support: Yellow neck hackle.
Tail: First, a red saddle, second, 2 green Flashabou, third, a turquoise saddle, fourth, 2 red Flashabou, fifth, a wide ginger saddle, sixth, 2 purple Flashabou, seventh, a wide red-brown saddle or neck hackle.
Body: Violet Mylar braid.
Collar: Bucktail, orange and light blue-gray on bottom and both sides.
Wing: Bucktail, orange and brown.
Cheeks: Lady Amherst pheasant tippets.
Eyes: Jungle cock.

Nighttime

Nighttime is a time when being alone
on the shoreline on the rocks or beach with the stars
or gray clouds or blackness of clouds with no moon,
can bring you so very close to full awareness
of the mystery of life that we are witness to.
I don't know why this is so and I never will know.
I feel it though, feel it so strongly when I walk in those places
where no one is, except me and other nocturnal beings.

I find the stars on those starry nights speak to me
in a place where there are no words, and yet I feel
an ache to know each of them,
a yearning to touch them somehow and
there is a strange emptiness in my stomach,
a vibration that isn't there and is nonetheless.
Then I see a familiar star and the mind grabs my awareness
and fixes it on the known. And a voice, I think it's mine,
says to no one in particular and me, "The Big Dipper! And where is
the North Star? Oh! There it is." And at that moment I spin around
and view another star that I do not know and welcome
my deliverence from that interruptive voice and
renew my wonder at it all again.

Some nights the clouds are strong and black and the blackness of the
sky and sea envelope me. In truth I am blind to light for there is none but
there is blackness and it is not all the same, and somehow,
I do not know why or how, I know where I am and where a fish may be.
And I know this is true. I know by the gentle tap he sends to me,
to the hand I have that he touches in response to my reaching out to
where he lays through my cast. This fish's touch makes it true.
In the blackness I see but not light, I see some other way that no one,
only nature, teaches and you can touch with this seeing
which cannot be described in words but can be felt somehow by all.

Gray nights are very different. They seem joyous late at night.
The eyes delight in night skies that are gray, not more than stars though.
All the same, gray skies at night are not like nights alone in blackness
or under starlight. They are kin to the day, to dawn and dusk and
are extensions of them in a way. The light lingers in them.
It does, although I do not know how this is true,
but it is somehow. And the fish are seen
in gray-skied nights and the feel of them is
different than in blackness or in starlight.
For fishing, I'll take the night.
It is so very much alive,
I'll take the night
and the awareness of the mystery
of all life and my life it brings.
It's the feel of it,
just the feel of it
and nothing more.

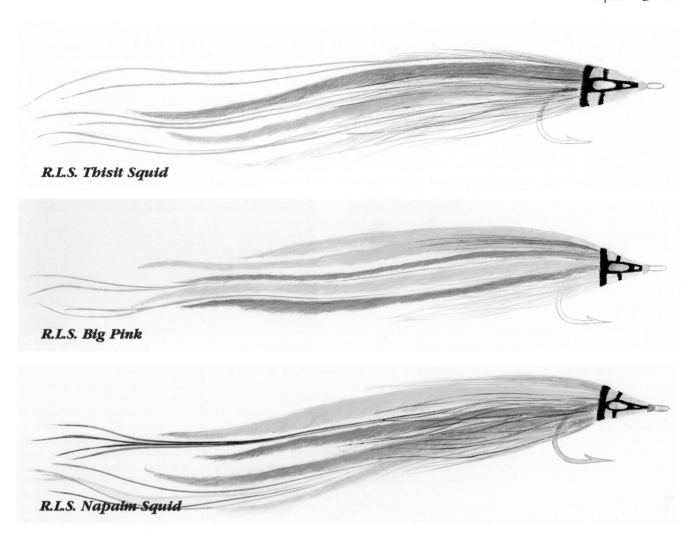

R.L.S. Thisit Squid

R.L.S. Big Pink

R.L.S. Napalm Squid

R.L.S. Thisit Squid

Hook: 253NA, Eagle Claw.
Thread: Yellow.
Platform: Light gray.
Pillow: Light gray.
Support: Light gray neck hackle.
Tail: First, a pale watery saddle, second, 2 silver Flashabou, third, a light blue gray saddle, fourth, 2 silver Flashabou, fifth, a wide, medium blue-gray saddle or neck hackle, 2 silver Flashabou.
Body: Silver Mylar braid.
Collar: Bucktail, light gray, bottom and both sides.
Wing: Bucktail, medium gray
Cheeks: First, 3 hairs each, pink, yellow, chartreuse, violet and orange, second, golden pheasant tippets, one on each side.
Eyes: Jungle cock.

R.L.S. Big Pink

Hook: 253NA, Eagle Claw.
Thread: Chartreuse.
Platform: Pink.
Pillow: Dubbing, chartreuse.
Support: Chartreuse neck hackle.
Tail: First, a silver doctor blue saddle, second, 2 pink Flashabou, third, a pink saddle, fourth, 2 light green Flashabou, fourth, an orange saddle, fifth, a pink saddle.
Body: Light green Mylar braid.
Collar: Bucktail, pink, bottom and both sides.
Wing: Bucktail, silver doctor blue.
Cheeks: First, 7 hairs of chartreuse, second, golden pheasant tippet.
Topping: A wide, pink saddle or neck feather.
Eyes: Jungle cock.

R.L.S. Napalm Squid

Hook: 253NA, Eagle Claw.
Thread: Orange.
Platform: Yellow.
Pillow: Yellow.
Support: Yellow neck hackle.
Tail: First, a ginger saddle, second, one strand each of red, gold, emerald green and silver Flashabou, third, a pumpkin saddle, fourth, an orange saddle, fifth, 2 blue and 2 purple Flashabou, sixth, a wide, yellow saddle.
Body: Silver Mylar braid.
Collar: Bucktail, yellow and light orange, bottom and both sides.
Wing: Bucktail, light blue and fluorescent yellow, mixed.
Cheeks: First, 5 hairs each, turquoise, violet, emerald green, second, golden pheasant tippet.
Eyes: Jungle cock.

CHAPTER 9

The Razzle Dazzle

Once upon a time my view of flies was centered on trying to duplicate the object I was trying to imitate. I did this for many years and tied many flies that caught fish well, then one day something in my way of looking at nature changed and I began to see flies differently. I experienced a shift in my perception, a paradigm shift, and no longer viewed flies as objects that should look exactly like replicas of what I was trying to imitate. Within a brief moment I realized that to fish, flies are perceived as living beings and even if they are perfect replicas to the human eye they may not catch fish because what a fish responds or reacts to in a fly is not exact physical likeness but the illusion of life.

This single realization changed my awareness and from that moment on, a new and powerful direction emerged in my fly tying, that of trying to create the illusion of life within the fly itself. The flies themselves were no longer seen as objects that a fish would either like or dislike but became a part of how I explored the fish's world. Flies lost their importance to me as patterns, and yet became much more important to me as illusions within the context of presentation. I realized that as long as I saw fish as having to make a decision to say yes to the fly in front of them, I was trying to overcome their natural caution.

I made a choice to approach the same situation from the opposite premise, which is, having them not say yes to the fly or ever engaging their natural caution. This meant not trying to attract them to the fly through some form of simulation but by allowing their natural predatory responses to be fully operational, which meant to me that if they don't say no to the fly or some part of its construction then they have automatically said yes to it. I wanted to see if I could create a fly that they would eat naturally without making a particular decision about the individual fly. I wanted them to eat it out of routine and I wanted it to fit into their routine like a placebo.

This approach to tying flies is not better than any other, it is a position that allows a minimalist view of fly tying to have a structure to create flies through elimination. It is similar to drawing a tree by drawing in the sky which surrounds it rather than drawing the leaves. The focus is on the space not on the leaves. This creates an image very different than one which is fixed only on the tree and disregards its surroundings. The image produced has space within and one can feel the sunlight and wind moving through, because there is room for them to be there. I try to replace every visual focal point with vagueness, for instance: silhouette instead of solid mass, length rather than thickness, transparency over opaqueness and space within the fly for the natural movement of materials by the water. Instead of constructing a solid sculptural replica or soft statue, I try to fashion a flexible mobile form; one that the fish can interpret as being alive because it is created to act and acts as if it were alive.

What this approach to tying does is make it possible to create a fly that swims and moves, that changes color with each and every motion and vibrates and flashes with the illusion of life from within. By choosing to diminish focal points rather than emphasizing them in effect you eliminate the possibility of a visual stimulation to the fish that he has to say yes to in order to strike. Because the fly acts naturally, and doesn't appear different than what the fish expects, he eats it.

Flies tied with these insights produce results that are truly amazing at first. Fish do not strike or hit them. They do, in fact, eat them. They are not fooled into overcoming their caution or mood by them. They accept them as food. They do not have to say yes, they already have.

I have often heard that large baitfish are difficult to imitate effectively. Actually, it all depends on how one thinks about imitation. Many fly tiers try to imitate large baitfish by making massive flies, i.e. stuffed animal flies, I imitate them through suggestion. My large flies are big but they are light and can be cast easily even with eight- and nine-weights. I have learned that proper placement of saddle hackles, along with small amounts of strategically located bits of bucktail and synthetics make flies that come to life by filling out in the water, breathe, move seeming from within and catch fish consistently.

I have one type of fly that I have been using for years that has proven its effectiveness over and over again, both to me and to my friends. Its name is Razzle Dazzle. I like this fly very much.

One June afternoon some years ago, I was fishing in Mount Hope Bay at the mouth of a tidal river for stripers. The tide had turned and was beginning to flood; the day was dark and had the exact right feel for striper fishing. I knew things were about to happen, it was just a matter of when.

This particular location fishes best on the flood tide, in fact it fishes best on the first surge of the flood. I walked to the edge of the water and made a few short casts cross-stream and fished them out with a wet-fly swing. I began to cast and fish down-current a step at a time, when I heard a whoosh sound in the water behind me. I turned in time to see a two-pound menhaden leap right towards me with a monster striper in hot pursuit. I'll make a long story short: I came back the next day an hour later to try again, and I brought along a very large new fly.

I made a few casts and liked the way the fly looked in the water, in fact I was surprised by how good it looked. It moved with every touch of current and when I moved my line or twitched my tip it shimmered with life. I knew right then and there that I had something good. I didn't know how good.

Right off the bat I missed five big fish in a row. They took the fly but I struck too soon and with the wrong method. Then I remembered a lesson I had learned in the late sixties and again in the early seventies; big stripers in current don't strike a lure they inhale it. I had been pulling the fly out of their mouth before they completed their take. When I felt the tap of a fish taking my fly I set the hook instinctively. The mistake I kept repeating was the tap I felt was not the fish's mouth closing on the fly, but the pull exerted on the fly when he flared his gills to suck it in. The next fish that hit I did hook; I did it by moving my tip toward the bank and waiting until the line came tight then set the hook, and the rest is history.

The Razzle Dazzle is tied to imitate large baitfish such as menhaden, blueback herring, alewives and if you vary the colors and materials, squid, mackerel or any other large forage fish you want to imitate. It is a

caricature of what you wish to imitate rather than a detailed painting or sculpture. This idea is important to understand.

The Razzle Dazzle works because it looks like a living creature when it is in the water. Out of the water it looks like any other slim streamer fly. It has the mass of the larger baitfish but only when in the water. The mass is an illusion caused by the water acting as an active ingredient or material within the fly itself. The placement of the saddle hackles and the thin bucktail collar causes the water itself to fill it out and form the shape it will take. It looks like a Deceiver at first glance, but it is not. It is tied differently and because the feathers are long and tied in flat and perfectly symmetrical it moves with a seductive side-to-side undulation. It is tied in layers of different-colored Mylar and different-colored feathers. This causes the colors to change hue as the light hits the feathers and the Mylar from different angles as the fly moves. When the fly is tied with yellow and blue hackle they will combine and reflect green but will still retain the yellow and blue color when viewed from a different angle. The Mylar gives off a subdued flash and the extension of the Mylar as a tail is extremely noticeable from a distance. The fly is balanced in silhouette, translucency, impressionism (as theory of color), movement and in its attractor qualities. It definitely appears to be alive in the water and it definitely catches big stripers.

This is one of my best big-fish flies. I tie it in many different color combinations but I always try to have all the primary colors present to some degree. The Mylar must extend past the tips of the saddle hackles by at least 3/4 of an inch. When you see this fly in the water you will know why it is named the Razzle Dazzle. Fish will leave a school of bait that they are actively feeding on to eat this fly. If you are hoping for a big fish then tie it seven inches long at the minimum, that seems to be the magic length for stripers over thirty pounds.

The way this fly is tied is caster-friendly. It can be cast without difficulty because it is not wind-resistant or bulky. If you tie it the way it is described, you will be able to cast easily, even with a seven-weight, as long as your leader is stiff enough and not too long.

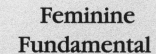

Feminine
Fundamental

I am always tying new flies. Most of them catch fish, but even so I often abandon and do not develop every successful fly into a series or theme. This is because I often get fresh insight and explore some other avenue or a much more intriguing idea comes along and I jump quickly to variations that may or may not be connected to the first idea. It makes no difference to me, just doing it is enough. The first fly is a sketch, like an artist's sketch. I try to get it down so that I can return and renew my focus if I have gone down a dead-end.

In order for me to stay with an idea or explore it to the end or as far as I can bring it, it must have an emotional side. If it is simply a technical process, say a new way of tying bodies for experimentation alone, I will not stick with it. Now, if I have the same idea but with the emotional energy of capturing the look and feel of a baitfish in a certain light, then I will not only do it but become lost in the doing of it and become oblivious to time passing by. The technical serves the emotional in me.

Technique is the track left when exploring a new path. Technique does not hold my interest for very long. It is routine and not the creative, although it is important it is the cart and not the horse. I know that if I follow my curiosity or interest in whatever it is that I find myself attracted to explore, I will find that the technique is following along and will have somehow magically developed along the way.

Fundamentals are all a teacher can offer. To be a good teacher you have to stick to the fundamentals. This old saw is also true in fly tying. There are no rules in fly tying, there are fundamentals and beauty and technique serves these. I have seen some technically perfect salmon flies that are not beautiful and I have seen others that are. What is the difference? Simple. The tier who ties beautiful flies seeks beauty and uses his feelings to capture or portray it. His technique is his footprint, it remains. The tier who focuses on rules sees rules and he must follow them to achieve his goal which is, of course, to create a masterpiece of fly-tying art. He see beauty but does not know that to give birth to beauty it must pass through you organically, it cannot be mechanical. The technique has mastered the tier and has kept him focused on method not on art. This approach is always less than fulfilling because the method stands in the way of touching and using the connection to feeling which inspired his desire to bring forth and portray the beauty that he loves. Attachment to technique can often stand in the way.

A fly that is an example of technical perfection may or may not be beautiful. If it appears to you as technically perfect at first glance then perhaps something is missing. A fly must have the look of life, the feel of being alive, the illusion of being. If it does not have this quality it is like a computer voice on the phone, something important is not there and this lack is disturbing, and interestingly the awareness of the lack comes through a feeling.

R.L.S. Razzle Dazzle

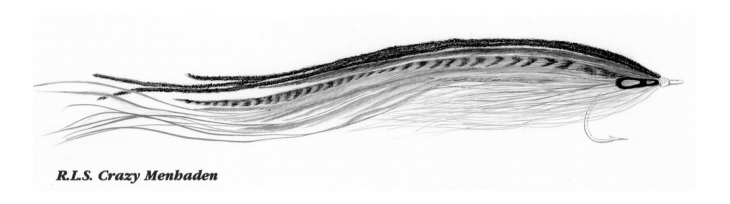

R.L.S. Crazy Menhaden

R.L.S. Razzle Dazzle

Length: As required.
Hook: 253NA, Eagle Claw, 1X short, all sizes.
Thread: White
Platform: Bucktail, white.
Pillow: Dubbing, white.
Support: White neck hackle tied curve side up.
Tail: First, three long white saddles tied flat, curve side down, one after the other, and 2 strands of gold Flashabou, third, one yellow saddle, fourth, 2 red Flashabou, fifth, silver doctor blue saddle, sixth, 2 silver Flashabou, seventh, a white saddle, eight, 2 light green Flashabou, ninth, a bright green saddle, tenth, 2 blue Flashabou. All the strands of Flashabou should extend at least 3/4 of an inch beyond the longest feather in the tail.
Body: Pearl or silver Mylar braid.
Collar: Long and fine white bucktail, tied as a veiling with a mix of several colors to produce a rainbow effect on the bottom and both sides. The collar should be very sparse and tied to flare slightly.
Wing: One long olive saddle, tied flat.
Topping: Short, 1 1/2-inch silver doctor fluorescent blue hackle tip tied flat.
Eyes: Jungle cock.

R.L.S. Crazy Menhaden

Length: As required.
Hook: 253NA, Eagle Claw, 1X short, all sizes.
Thread: Beige.
Platform: Bucktail: orange and yellow.
Pillow: Dubbing, ginger.
Support: Ginger neck hackle, curve side up.
Tail: First, 2 copper Flashabou, second, a ginger saddle followed by a pink then a yellow, third, 2 copper Flashabou, fourth, a cantaloupe saddle, fifth, 2 red Flashabou, sixth, a pink saddle, seventh, a violet saddle, eighth, a pink saddle, ninth, a chartreuse saddle, tenth, 2 emerald green Flashabou, eleventh, a blue saddle followed by a red grizzly.
Body: Gold Mylar braid.
Collar: Bucktail, beige on the bottom, yellow and beige mixed on the sides.
Wing: First, small amount of orange bucktail, 15 to 20 hairs, followed by long, wide olive saddle.
Cheeks: Bucktail, 3 hairs each, orange, turquoise, chartreuse, emerald green.
Topping: 7 strands of peacock herl (optional).
Eyes: Jungle cock.

The Moment

A fly is an expression of something intangible, something indefinable.
The fly can never completely embody the intangible quality I am talking about,
it can only be a part of its expression. A fly is a part of presentation.

The water I am fishing in has to be considered and the fish I wish to catch has to be
thought about also. The type of line is critical as is the leader and how it will lead the fly
through the water. The line leads the leader and the rod leads the line and it all extends from me,
the fisherman. The hook that the fly is tied on is important for having the fly swim or suspend
as need be, and the hair and feathers have to be fashioned so they will do what they should.

The cast I make will be to the place it needs to be so that if I need to mend or feed line
I will be in good position to do it effortlessly. I will need to mend line for the fly to act correctly
if I am trying to catch a particular fish, which I will be doing.

The line will float because I want the control that a floating line provides in fishing a fly
with presentation as the focus. The fly will have to be made in a way that it looks and acts
as if it were meandering along, letting the current carry it while it swims lazily,
just like a slowly undulating creature. It will have to have the feel of life tied into it
because of the way I will fish it. I will fish it in harmony with the current and let the current
carry it to where a fish is waiting for just this very creature to come meandering along.

I won't strip the fly, I will tighten the line and twitch my tip from time to time and
I will follow this by feeding some held line into the drift, and let the fly slowly sink or drop
a foot or so. The hook will be light and this is so the fly will descend slowly and not dive but glide.
Then I will mend and tighten and mend again. As the fly comes to where I wish a fish to be,
I lean forward slightly and lead the fly with just a bit of pressure. Just enough to be awake
to the danger that if it were what it appeared to be, it would now be aware of, I may twitch it,
I may let it settle. This is the moment I am moving towards, this particular moment. If the fish comes
it will be gentle, a slight tap is all it will be, and when I tighten I will know how big he is,
even if he is a she and if there is no fish, I will feel good about the cast, the mends, the hook.
I will cast again and fish it through. Perhaps the same, perhaps not, and when that moment
of tightening my body and leaning forward just a little comes again, perhaps this time the tap will come.

I remember this every time I fish a fly that has to swim as if it were alive and more.

R.L.S. Hurricane

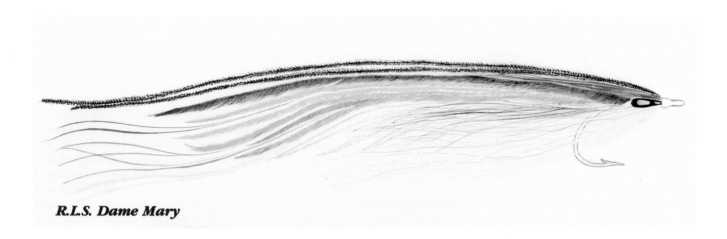

R.L.S. Dame Mary

R.L.S. Hurricane

Length: As required.
Hook: 253NA, Eagle Claw, 1X short, all sizes.
Thread: White.
Platform: Bucktail, chartreuse topped with orange.
Pillow: Dubbing, chartreuse.
Support: Chartreuse neck hackle.
Tail: First, two white saddles followed by apple green saddle, second, 2 violet Flashabou, third, a pink saddle then a light blue one, fourth, 2 copper Flashabou, fifth, a yellow saddle, sixth, 2 gold Flashabou, seventh, an orange saddle, eighth, 2 emerald green Flashabou, ninth, a natural red grizzly followed by another natural red grizzly.
Body: Light green Mylar braid.
Collar: Bucktail, light ginger on bottom, pale yellow on sides.
Wing: Bucktail, light tan and light olive mixed.
Cheeks: Bucktail, 4 hairs of orange, 4 hairs of turquoise, 4 hairs of chartreuse.
Eyes: Jungle cock.

R.L.S. Dame Mary

Length: As required.
Hook: 253NA, Eagle Claw, 1X short, all sizes.
Thread: White.
Platform: Bucktail, fluorescent white.
Pillow: Dubbing, fluorescent white.
Support: Fluorescent white neck hackle.
Tail: First, three fluorescent white saddles, second, 2 pearl Flashabou, third, a ginger saddle, fourth, 2 silver Flashabou, fifth, a ginger saddle, sixth, 2 light green Flashabou, seventh, a yellow saddle, eighth, a fluorescent yellow saddle, ninth, 2 red Flashabou, tenth, a chartreuse saddle followed by an olive saddle.
Body: Silver Mylar braid.
Collar: Bucktail, fluorescent white on bottom, ginger on sides.
Wing: Bucktail, light olive.
Cheeks: Bucktail, 3 hairs each, turquoise, pink, violet, emerald green and fluorescent yellow.
Topping: Seven strands of peacock herl.
Eyes: Jungle cock.

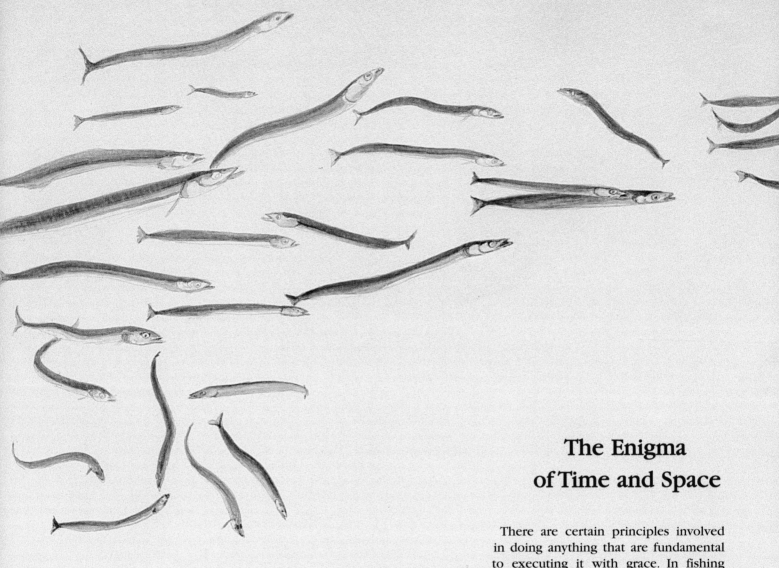

The Enigma
of Time and Space

There are certain principles involved in doing anything that are fundamental to executing it with grace. In fishing there are many such fundamentals. Casting a fly rod is one, tying knots is another, they are procedures or skills that we learn by doing. There are other fundamental skills that are not often mentioned, such as reading the water, tying a fly with balance, choosing the right thickness of leader to make a fly swim correctly, imagining where a fish will hold and how to cast to bring the fly to his world. The list is endless and it gets more and more detailed as one learns more and more of the language of the mechanics of fly fishing.

There are mechanics in anything from ballet to digging a ditch. Understanding mechanics can often be a doorway to executing complicated, seemingly impossible procedures with magical grace. It's finding the lowest common denominator, the root, the point of origin, the basic core of balance in what we are doing. It can be as simple as fishing where the fish are instead of casting a beautiful long line all day and all night where they never will be. All the mechanics of fly fishing can be reduced to a single root principle. There is one fundamental truth that can reduce every beautiful theory, every scientific fact about fish and fishing to irreducible irrelevance. It's one of those self-evident truths we prefer to ignore, "You simply can't catch a fish where he ain't."

R.L.S. Rosey Mack

R.L.S. Striper Moon

R.L.S. Rosey Mack

Length: As required.

Hook: 253NA, Eagle Claw, 1X short, all sizes.

Thread: Yellow.

Platform: Bucktail, yellow.

Pillow: Dubbing, yellow.

Support: Yellow neck hackle, curve side up.

Tail: First, 2 gold Flashabou, second, one white saddle followed by two ginger saddles, third, 2 red Flashabou, fourth, a violet saddle, fifth, a wide gray saddle, sixth, a ginger saddle, seventh, a yellow grizzly saddle, eighth, 2 silver Flashabou, ninth, a turquoise grizzly saddle, tenth, 2 green Flashabou, eleventh, a yellow grizzly, twelfth, a chartreuse grizzly.

Body: Pearl Mylar braid.

Collar: Bucktail, white on the bottom, white and pink on the sides.

Wing: Bucktail, emerald green, black, yellow, mixed.

Cheeks: Bucktail, 3 hairs each, fluorescent yellow, fluorescent turquoise, orange, violet.

Topping: 7 strands of peacock herl (optional, but nice).

Eyes: Jungle cock.

R.L.S. Striper Moon

Length: As required.

Hook: 253NA, Eagle Claw, 1X short, all sizes.

Thread: White.

Platform: White.

Pillow: Dubbing, white.

Support: White neck hackle.

Tail: First, three white saddles, second, 2 pearl Flashabou, third, a yellow saddle, 2 pearl Flashabou, fourth, a pink saddle, fifth, a violet saddle, sixth, 2 red Flashabou, seventh, a violet saddle, eighth, 2 purple Flashabou, ninth, a pink saddle, tenth, 2 gold Flashabou, eleventh, a turquoise saddle, twelfth, a light purple saddle (more blue than red), thirteenth, 2 red Flashabou, fourteenth, a deep-blue saddle followed by an olive saddle.

Body: Violet pearl Mylar.

Collar: Bucktail, white on bottom, violet and yellow mixed on sides.

Wing: Bucktail, light blue and violet mixed.

Cheeks: Bucktail, 3 hairs each, yellow, chartreuse, violet, turquoise and orange.

Topping: Seven strands of peacock herl.

Eyes: Jungle cock.

CHAPTER 10

Additional Fly Patterns

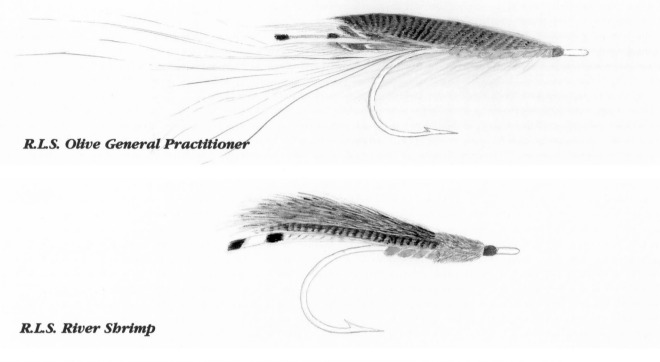

R.L.S. Olive General Practitioner

R.L.S. River Shrimp

R.L.S. Black General Practitioner

R.L.S. Olive General Practitioner
Hook: 253NA,
Antennae: Olive bucktail.
Head: Ring-necked pheasant rump feather (short).
Eyes: Golden pheasant tippet.
Body: Light gray wool.
Ribbing: Gold oval tinsel.
Hackle: Pale watery dun (light gray).
Carapace: Ring-necked pheasant rump feather.
Back: Dyed mallard, medium olive.
Tail: Dyed mallard, light olive.

R.L.S. River Shrimp
Hook: Any light wire 2X long, carbon steel hook.
Tail: Barred wood duck or golden pheasant tippet.
Underbody: Gold or silver flat tinsel.
Overbody: Amber Swannundaze.
Underwing: Bronze mallard.
Overwing: Gray fox or woodchuck guard hair.
Head: Spun deer hair clipped flat on the bottom and very short. The top and sides are clipped short and angled back to conform to the shape of the tail section of a shrimp.

This fly can be greased to suspend in or just under the surface film, and is effective when fished with a dead-drift or greased-line presentation.

R.L.S. Black General Practitioner
Hook: 253NA, Eagle Claw.
Antennae: Black and blue bucktail.
Head: Black golden pheasant neck feather.
Eyes: Golden pheasant tippet.
Body: Gold flat tinsel
Ribbing: Gold oval tinsel.
Hackle: Natural black.
Carapace: Metallic black turkey feather.
Back: Same.
Tail: Same.

Note: A variation of the original B.G.P. a West Coast steelhead fly.

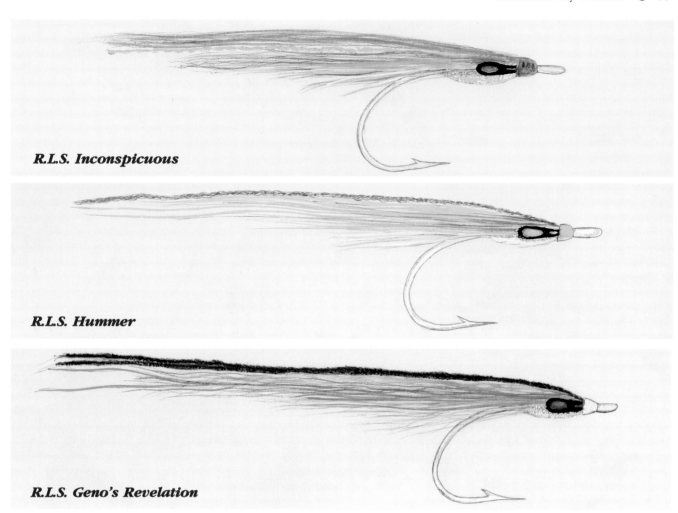

R.L.S. Inconspicuous

R.L.S. Hummer

R.L.S. Geno's Revelation

R.L.S. Inconspicuous

Length: Tiny to large.
Hook: 253 NA, Eagle Claw.
Thread: Tan.
Tail: None:
Body: Yellow pearl Mylar braid.
Wing: Bucktail, 10 hairs of white, 10 hairs of ginger, 1 1/2 times length of hook, mixed, under 10 hairs of pink, 10 hairs of ginger, 5 hairs of apple green 2 times the length of the hook, mixed, under 2 strands of yellow Krystal Flash, under 10 hairs of tan, 5 hairs of light gray, 4 hairs of orange, 8 hairs of olive, mixed, 2 1/2 times the length of the hook.
Topping: None.
Eyes: Jungle cock.

R.L.S. Hummer

Length: Tiny to large.
Hook: 253 NA, Eagle Claw.
Tail: None:
Body: Pearl Mylar braid.
Wing: Bucktail, 10 hairs of white, 4 hairs of pink, 4 hairs of apple green 1 1/2 times the length of the hook, mixed, under 10 hairs of golden yellow and light orange 2 1/2 times the length of the hook, mixed, under 2 strips of green Flashabou one inch longer than the wing, under 8 hairs each of fluorescent yellow, medium yellow and light yellow 3 1/2 times the length of the hook, mixed.
Cheeks: 3 hairs each of turquoise blue and emerald green tied full length as color accents on both sides of the fly.
Topping: 4 strands of light blue Krystal Flash tied as long as the Flashabou. Optional: 7 strands of peacock herl tied as long as, and on top of, the Krystal Flash.
Eyes: Jungle cock.

R.L.S. Geno's Revelation

Length: Tiny to large.
Hook: 253NA, Eagle Claw, all sizes.
Thread: White.
Tail: None.
Body: Silver or pearl Mylar braid.
Wing: Bucktail, 15 hairs of white, 15 hairs of light amber mixed, 1 1/2 times length of hook under 10 hairs of chartreuse, 15 hairs of light blue, 8 hairs of pink mixed, 2 times length of hook, under two strips of pink Flashabou one inch longer than the wing, under 15 hairs of pale apple green, 10 hairs of Silver Doctor blue mixed, 2 1/2 times the length of the hook.
Topping: Seven strands of peacock herl one half inch longer than the wing.
Eyes: Jungle cock.

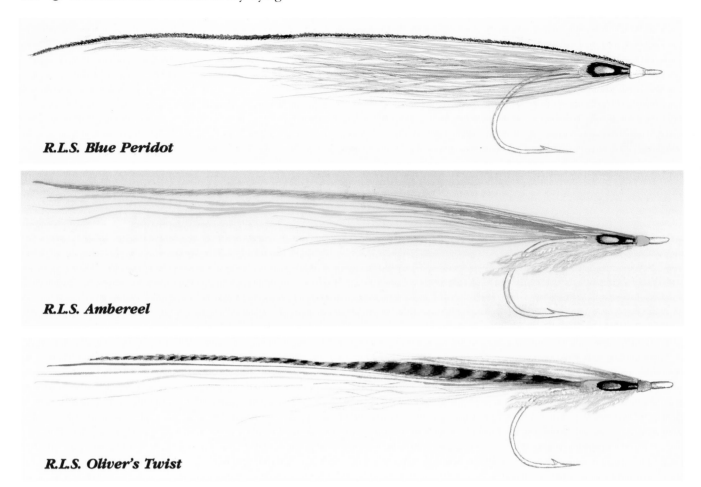

R.L.S. Blue Peridot

R.L.S. Ambereel

R.L.S. Oliver's Twist

R.L.S. Blue Peridot

Length: As required.
Hook: 253NA, Eagle Claw, 1X short, all sizes.
Thread: White.
Platform: Bucktail, 20 long hairs of pink, 10 long hairs of fluorescent yellow mixed.
Tail: One long, medium wide pale turquoise saddle, flat, curve side down.
Body: Gold or green Mylar braid.
Collar: Bucktail, 50 hairs light blue, 2 1/2 times the length of the hook spread to surround the bottom 2/3 of the body and flow back and merge with the tail.
Wing: Bucktail, 30 hairs of chartreuse 3x the length of the hook.
Cheeks: Bucktail, 5 Hairs of medium orange, fanned on each side, not a clump, as long as the collar.
Topping: Seven strands of peacock herl 1/2 inch longer than the whole fly.
Eyes: Jungle cock.

R.L.S. Ambereel

Length: As required.
Hook: 253NA, Eagle Claw, 1X short, all sizes.
Thread: Yellow.
Platform: Bucktail, 30 hairs light beige.
Tail: 3 strips Flashabou, 2 gold, 1 green, under 1 long narrow pumpkin saddle, tied flat curve side down.
Body: Gold Mylar braid.
Throat: Light beige marabou, vee cut, tied under shank as veiling, as long as hook.
Wing: Bucktail, 30 hairs pumpkin 2 1/2 times the length of the hook, or, 15 hairs light, beige, 7 hairs orange, 7 hairs pale yellow, 2 1/2 times the length of the hook mixed.
Eyes: Jungle cock.

R.L.S. Oliver's Twist

Length: As required.
Hook: 253NA, Eagle Claw, 1X short, all sizes.
Thread: Olive.
Platform: Bucktail, 30 hairs of pale gray.
Tail: 4 stands of Flashabou, 1 silver, 1 gold, 1 blue, 1 red under one long, narrow, thin stemmed olive grizzly saddle hackle, tied flat, curve down.
Body: Gold Mylar braid.
Throat: Light beige marabou, as long as the hook, bottom and both sides (vee cut).
Wing: Bucktail, 15 hairs light gray, 15 hairs olive, 2 times the length of the hook, mixed.
Cheeks: Bucktail, 1 hair each of emerald green, turquoise, orange and chartreuse, tied as a clump on each side, as long as the wing, just below the wing. (Topping: Seven strands of peacock herl.
Eyes: Jungle cock.

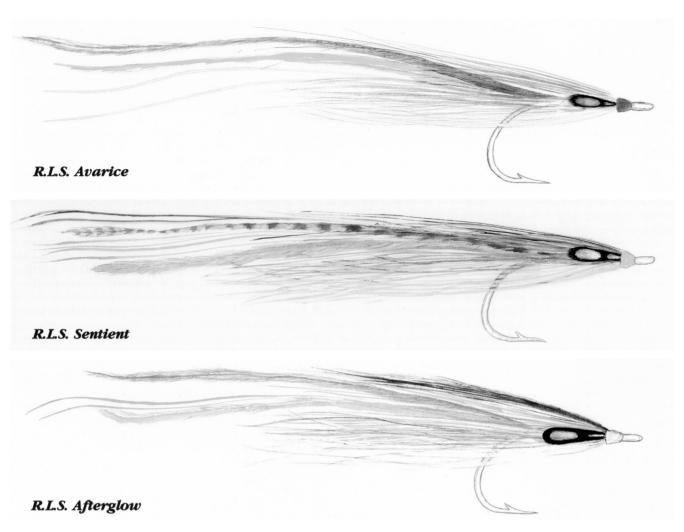

R.L.S. Avarice

R.L.S. Sentient

R.L.S. Afterglow

R.L.S. Avarice
Length: As required.
Hook: 253NA, Eagle Claw, 1X short, all sizes.
Thread: Olive.
Platform: Bucktail, 30 hairs light blue.
Tail: 2 strips of pink Flashabou, under 1 long yellow saddle under 1 long light olive saddle.
Body: Light green Mylar braid.
Collar: Bucktail, 2 times the length of the hook, tied to veil the bottom of the body, bottom section, 20 hairs of pale pastel green, sides, 10 hairs of apple green.
Wing: Bucktail, 5 hairs of chartreuse, 5 hairs orange, 20 hairs of light olive, mixed 2 1/2 times the length of the hook.
Cheeks: Bucktail, 4 hairs ginger, fanned on each side.
Eyes: Jungle cock.

R.L.S. Sentient
Length: As required.
Hook: 253NA, Eagle Claw, 1X short, all sizes.
Thread: Yellow.
Platform: Bucktail, 30 yellow under 10 orange.
Tail: One ginger saddle under 4 strips of Flashabou, 1 light blue, 1 gold, 1 pink, 1 chartreuse, under one natural red grizzly under 2 strips of copper Flashabou.
Body: Gold.
Collar: Bucktail, light beige, bottom 2/3 of the hook, 2 1/2 times the length of the hook. Wing: Bucktail, 5 hairs of orange, 5 hairs of dark cordovan brown, 15 tan 10 olive, mixed, 3 times the length of the hook.
Cheeks: Bucktail, 2 hairs of orange, 2 chartreuse, 2 turquoise, 2 pink as long as the wing.
Eyes: Jungle cock.

R.L.S. Afterglow
Length: As required.
Hook: 253NA, Eagle Claw, 1X short, all sizes.
Thread: White.
Platform: Bucktail, 30 hairs white, 10 hairs of yellow on top.
Tail: One chartreuse saddle under 2 strips of gold Flashabou under one turquoise saddle under 2 strips of violet Flashabou.
Body: Yellow pearl Mylar braid.
Collar: Bucktail, sides light violet 2 times the length of the hook, tied to surround the bottom 2/3 of the body.
Wing: Bucktail, 20 hairs turquoise under 10 hairs of dark blue, 10 hairs of purple mixed.
Cheeks: Bucktail, 3 hairs of chartreuse, as long as the wing.
Eyes: Jungle cock.

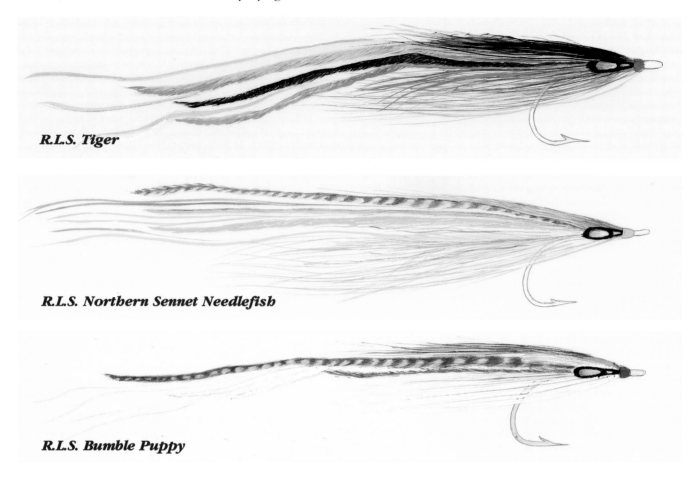

R.L.S. Tiger

R.L.S. Northern Sennet Needlefish

R.L.S. Bumble Puppy

R.L.S. Tiger

Length: As required.
Hook: 253NA, Eagle Claw, 1X short, all sizes.
Thread: Orange.
Platform: Bucktail, cantaloupe or a mix of orange and yellow.
Pillow: Feather dubbing.
Support: Cantaloupe neck hackle curve side up.
Tail: First one cantaloupe saddle, second, 2 strips of gold Flashabou, third, one black saddle, fourth, 2 strips of gold Flashabou, fifth, one cantaloupe saddle, sixth, 2 strips of gold Flashabou.
Body: Gold Mylar braid.
Collar: Bucktail, cantaloupe or orange and yellow mixed, tied to surround the bottom 2/3 of the body and flared slightly by tightening the thread.
Wing: Bucktail, black.
Cheeks: Bucktail, 3 hairs of turquoise, 3 hairs emerald green.
Eyes: Jungle cock.

R.L.S. Northern Sennet Needlefish

Length: Very long.
Hook: 253 NA, Eagle Claw.
Thread: Yellow.
Platform: Bucktail, ginger under orange.
Pillow: Dubbing, pale green.
Support: Pale green neck hackle.
Tail: first, 2 strips light green Flashabou, second, yellow saddle, third, 2 strips of gold Flashabou, fourth, ginger saddle, fifth, 2 strips of copper Flashabou, sixth, natural red grizzly saddle. Flashabou to extend 1 inch beyond wing. Body: Gold Mylar braid.
Collar: Bucktail, ginger. (light yellowish buff)
Wing: Bucktail, yellow, orange, with a little bit of reddish brown or olive to darken the wing slightly.
Cheeks: Bucktail, 12 hairs, 3 apple green, 3 turquoise, 3 pink, 3 violet, fanned.
Eyes: Jungle cock.

R.L.S. Bumble Puppy

Length: As required.
Hook: 253 NA, Eagle Claw.
Thread: White or red.
Platform: Bucktail, white.
Pillow: Dubbing, white.
Support: White or red neck hackle.
Tail: First, white saddle, second, 2 strips of pearl Flashabou, third, white saddle, fourth, 2 strips of silver Flashabou, fifth, natural red grizzly.
Body: White and red chenille spiraled or white chenille with a red chenille rib.
Collar: Bucktail, white.
Wing: Bucktail: small bunch of white bucktail cut off blunt just above the bend of the hook under ginger, brown and tan bucktail blended to mimic the coloration of the red grizzly hackle used in the tail, 2 1/2 times hook length.
Cheeks: Bucktail, 5 hairs red each side.
Eyes: Jungle cock.

R.L.S. Mutable Squid

R.L.S. Orange and Blue Squidazzle

R.L.S. Indigo Squid

R.L.S. Mutable Squid

Hook: 253NA, Eagle Claw.
Thread: Gray.
Platform: Light gray.
Pillow: Gray.
Support: Gray neck hackle.
Tail: First, a medium-gray saddle, second, a ginger saddle, third, 4 pearl Flashabou, fourth, a pink saddle, fifth, 5 strands of Flashabou one each, red, gold, blue, emerald green and purple, sixth, a medium-gray saddle.
Body: Light blue Mylar braid.
Collar: Bucktail, medium gray, bottom and both sides.
Wing: Bucktail, medium gray.
Cheeks: First, 3 hairs each, orange, turquoise, chartreuse, violet and pink, second, Lady Amherst pheasant tippets, one on each side.
Eyes: Jungle cock.

R.L.S. Orange and Blue Squidazzle

Length: Squid grow to over twelve inches.
Hook: 253NA, Eagle Claw.
Thread: Orange.
Platform: Orange and blue bucktail.
Pillow: Dubbing, yellow.
Support: Yellow neck hackle tied curve or dull side up.
Tail: First, a silver doctor blue saddle, second, 2 red Flashabou, third, a fire orange saddle, fourth, 2 emerald green Flashabou, fifth, a fire orange saddle, sixth, 2 gold Flashabou, seventh, a long, wide fiery brown saddle or neck hackle, eighth, 2 blue Flashabou.
Body: Light violet body braid.
Wing: Fire orange saddle under light violet saddle.
Collar: Bucktail, orange tied to flare slightly.
Cheeks: Bucktail, 5 hairs each, turquoise, chartreuse, and yellow.
Eyes: Jungle cock.

R.L.S. Indigo Squid

Hook: 253NA, Eagle Claw.
Thread: Black.
Platform: Orange.
Pillow: Dubbing, deep blue.
Support: Deep blue neck hackle.
Tail: First, a purple saddle, second, 2 pearl Flashabou, third, a violet saddle, fourth, 2 silver Flashabou., fifth, a wide, deep-blue saddle, sixth, an orange saddle.
Body: Silver Mylar braid.
Collar: Bucktail, medium and deep blue, bottom and both sides.
Wing: First, medium-blue bucktail, second, a wide, deep-blue saddle.
Cheeks: First, 5 hairs of orange bucktail, second, Lady Amherst tippets.
Topping: 10 hairs of deep-blue bucktail.
Eyes: Jungle cock.

R.L.S. Blue Dog Bonita

R.L.S. Moby Dick

R.L.S. Blue Dog Bonita

Length: As required.

Hook: 253NA, Eagle Claw, 1X short, all sizes.

Thread: White.

Platform: Pink.

Pillow: Dubbing, pink.

Support: Pink neck hackle.

Tail: First, three pink saddles, second, 2 pearl Flashabou, third, a white saddle, fourth, 2 silver Flashabou, fifth, a light blue saddle, sixth, 2 light blue Flashabou, seventh, a light blue saddle, eighth, a yellow saddle, ninth, 2 emerald green Flashabou, tenth, a white saddle, eleventh, a chartreuse saddle, 12th, a yellow saddle.

Body: Rose pearl Mylar braid.

Collar: Bucktail, pink on bottom, light blue on sides.

Wing: Bucktail, yellow.

Cheeks: Bucktail, 3 hairs each, turquoise, chartreuse, red and violet.

Topping: Bucktail, 4 hairs of dark blue and 4 hairs of emerald green.

Eyes: Jungle cock.

R.L.S. Moby Dick

Length: As required.

Hook: 253NA, Eagle Claw, 1X short, all sizes.

Thread: White.

Platform: Bucktail, fluorescent white.

Pillow: Dubbing, white.

Support: White neck hackle.

Tail: First, 2 pearl Flashabou, second, three fluorescent white saddles, one on top of the other, third, 2 pearl Flashabou, fourth, a pink saddle, fifth, 2 pink Flashabou, fifth, a violet saddle, sixth, a pink saddle, seventh, 2 pearl Flashabou, eighth, a fluorescent white saddle, ninth, another fluorescent white saddle, tenth, 4 strips of Flashabou one each, light blue, light green, pink, light violet, eleventh, a pale blue-gray saddle.

Body: Pearl Mylar braid.

Collar: Bucktail, fluorescent white, bottom and both sides.

Wing: Bucktail, pale gray.

Cheeks: Bucktail, 3 hairs each, pink, fluorescent yellow, chartreuse, turquoise and violet.

Topping: Seven strands of peacock herl (optional).

Eyes: Jungle cock.

R.L.S. Scuptaug

R.L.S. Pink Needlefish

R.L.S. Scuptaug

Length: As required.

Hook: 253NA, Eagle Claw, 1X short, all sizes.

Thread: Yellow.

Platform: Bucktail, light ginger.

Pillow: Ginger dubbing.

Support: Ginger neck hackle.

Tail: First, three ginger saddles, second, a yellow saddle, third, 2 copper Flashabou, fourth, a chartreuse saddle, fifth, 2 red Flashabou, sixth, a medium-gray saddle, seventh, 2 silver Flashabou, eighth, a yellow saddle followed by an orange saddle followed by a fiery brown saddle.

Body: Gold Mylar braid.

Collar: Bucktail, light ginger on bottom, tan on both sides.

Wing: Bucktail, medium brown with a reddish cast.

Cheeks: Bucktail, 3 hairs each, orange, yellow, chartreuse and red.

Eyes: Jungle cock.

R.L.S. Pink Needlefish

Length: As required.

Hook: 253NA, Eagle Claw, 1X short, all sizes.

Thread: White.

Platform: Fluorescent white bucktail.

Pillow: Light gray dubbing.

Support: Fluorescent white neck hackle.

Tail: First, a fluorescent white saddle, second, 2 pearl Flashabou, third, a pale gray saddle, fourth, 2 blue pearl Flashabou, fifth, a light blue-gray saddle, sixth, 2 rose pearl Flashabou, seventh, a ginger saddle, eighth, 2 gold Flashabou, ninth, a pink saddle, tenth, 2 blue pearl Flashabou, eleventh, a pink saddle.

Body: Pearl Mylar braid.

Collar: Bucktail, pale gray on bottom, light ginger on sides.

Wing: Bucktail, pink and light gray mixed.

Cheeks: Bucktail, 2 hairs each, turquoise, orange, chartreuse and violet.

Eyes: Jungle cock.

R.L.S. Rat a Tat

R.L.S. Orange Aide

R.L.S. Rat a Tat
Length: As required.
Hook: 253NA, Eagle Claw, 1X short, all sizes.
Thread: Chartreuse.
Platform: Black
Pillow: Chartreuse dubbing.
Support: Chartreuse neck hackle.
Tail: First, yellow grizzly saddle, second, a chartreuse saddle, third, 2 red Flashabou, fourth, a turquoise grizzly saddle, fifth, a light blue saddle, sixth, 2 gold Flashabou, seventh, a yellow grizzly saddle, eighth, a ginger saddle, ninth, 2 emerald green Flashabou, tenth, a fluorescent green grizzly, eleventh, 2 red Flashabou, twelfth, a yellow grizzly.
Body: Gold Mylar braid.
Collar: Bucktail, ginger, bottom and both sides.
Wing: Bucktail, yellow.
Cheeks: Bucktail, 3 hairs each, turquoise, orange, chartreuse, dark blue and emerald green.
Topping: Seven strands of peacock herl.
Eyes: Jungle cock.

R.L.S. Orange Aide
Length: As required.
Hook: 253NA, Eagle Claw, 1X short, all sizes.
Thread: Yellow.
Platform: Yellow.
Pillow: Dubbing, yellow.
Support: Yellow neck hackle.
Tail: First, a ginger saddle, second, 2 gold Flashabou, third, an orange saddle, fourth, a ginger saddle, fifth, 2 red Flashabou, sixth, a yellow saddle, seventh, an orange saddle, eighth, 2 copper Flashabou, ninth, a wide, medium-brown saddle.
Body: Gold Mylar braid.
Collar: Bucktail, ginger on bottom, orange and yellow mixed on sides.
Wing: Bucktail, ginger.
Cheeks: Bucktail, 4 hairs turquoise, 4 hairs violet.
Topping: Bucktail, 8 hairs of emerald green, 3 hairs of dark blue.
Eyes: Jungle cock.

CHAPTER 11

Witnessing

"Fishing is the contemplative man's sport."
From the first book ever written about fly fishing,
Treatyse of Fysshynge Wyth An Angle—Dame Julian Berners, 14th Century

The ocean is so very big and so very mysterious. When I think about what I have seen and felt while exploring it, it makes me laugh at how insignificant my experience truly is, and yet I am thoroughly content with my portion. I will never know more than I can know and that will never be more than a scratch on its surface, and maybe not even that. I could spend many lifetimes and never be much further along in my knowledge of the ocean than where I am now, but it would be fun and not boring ever.

A river is much the same in terms of vastness of mystery. It is a mystery for sure. Sometimes I remember watching rainwater flow downhill when I was a boy. I have many memories of this. Visions of puddles flowing out and watching the sand move and form tiny sand bars and oxbows, and I remember knowing that rivers all did this. I still look at puddles and the water flowing out of them. I am always struck by my lack of thought while I am focused on this. It is as if my inner dialogue shuts off totally and there is no time. I don't lose track of time, there is only the present. I never know afterwards if I have been watching the flow for

thirty seconds or thirty minutes, it feels the same to me, funny how that is. There is no awareness of time when you shut off the inner dialogue and step outside of its restraints. Moving water is remarkable in its power to attract and transfix and transport our attention. I wonder where it takes us when we let it carry our awareness along in its flow. Perhaps the Ancients were talking about this property of water when they said that there were four elements, Earth, Air, Fire and Water. Water certainly has other properties than physical ones.

I do miss a lot. Perhaps I miss almost all of what is truly there to witness if I could be aware and just present to its unfolding. I see what I see and I have seen marvels unfold before my eyes. I have been fortunate and grateful for the small view that I have had. I hope that it grows; if I am as all other men are, it will for we are all gifted with some share of awe at the mystery that we are a part of and somehow mysteriously reflect. The unknown becomes the known and reveals more unknown, it never ends and I can only see and feel to the depth of my willingness to witness and wonder at it all.

There Is More

"In the pursuit of knowledge everyday something is added.
In the pursuit of wisdom everyday something is dropped."

Lao Tsu, circa 2500 BC

Fishing can be practiced in many ways
and practice is preparation
For me fishing is an art
When I witness a fisherman who is fishing from his heart
I watch
I watch because it is a performance
it is not practice, it is empowerment
It is within and without
It is full of grace
It is not casting or measuring up to others
It is not about pretense or posturing
It is free and flowing
It is harmony, balance
It is not contained in dogma or equipment
it is not just about fish.

It is man in his fullness as the being who is aware
and perceives with more than any one part of himself
It is the natural spirit of man set free from cultural limitation
It is engagement with his totality
It is primal and singular and it is a dance of spirit.

The spirit of man and the spirit of fish
preformed and choreographed and directed
by the power that is mystery itself.

RECOMMENDED READING

Bergman, Ray. *Trout.* New York, New York: Alfred A. Knopf

Gifford, Tom. *Anglers and Muscleheads.* New York, New York: E.P. Dutton & Co., Inc., 1960

Jorgensen, Poul. *Salmon flies their Character, Style, and Dressing.* Harrisburg, Pennsylvania: Stackpole Books, 1978

Ferguson, Bruce. Les Johnson, Pat Trotter. *Fly Fishing for Pacific Salmon.* Portland, Oregon: Frank Amato Publications, Inc., 1985

Kreh, Lefty. *Fly Fishing in Salt Water.* New York, New York: Crown Publishers, Inc., 1974

Scott, Jock. *Greased Line Fishing (for Salmon and Steelhead).* Portland, Oregon: Frank Amato Publications, Inc., 1982

Haig-Brown, Roderick. Every book he ever wrote especially, *A River Never Sleeps.*

Sylvester, Jerry. *Saltwater Fishing is Easy.* Harrisburg, Pennsylvania: Stackpole Books, 1956.

McMillan, Bill. *Dry Line Steelhead.* Portland, Oregon: Frank Amato Publications, Inc., 1987 (Out of print)

Nemes, Slyvester. *The Soft Hackled Fly.* Old Greenwich, Connecticut: The Chatham Press, 1975

Bondorow, Ray. *Stripers and Streamers.* Portland Oregon: Frank Amato Publications, Inc., 1996

Gartside, Jack. *Striper Strategies.* Boston, Massachusetts: Self-published, 1997

Tabory, Lou. *Inshore Fly Fishing.* New York, New York: Lyons & Burford, 1994

Wyeth, Andrew. *Two Worlds of Andrew Wyeth: The Kuerners and Olsons.* New York, New York: Metropolitan Museum of Art Bulletin, 1976

Abrames, J. Kenney. *Striper Moon.* Portland Oregon: Frank Amato Publications, Inc., 1994

R.L.S. stands for *Roccus Leneatus Saxatilis,*
the old latin name for striped bass
which seems to reflect the spirit of the fish
much better than the modern latin name.
A perfect name for a perfect fish.

INDEX OF FLY PATTERNS

INDEX OF VIGNETTES

INDEX OF ARTWORK